D0168095

"A meditation on memory and history . . . In this slim but powerful book, Sebald has once again shown that he belongs in the upper echelon of those writers working at the turn of the twenty-first century."   —*Orlando Sentinel*

"[Sebald's] great achievement is to have shown the way. In a world of transgression, where science, technology, and for that matter terrorism devastate definition, former categories—be they history, fiction, memory, language, image, or illusion—lose validity and can in fact become restrictive. W. G. Sebald sought to point this out."

—*The New York Sun*

On the Natural History
of Destruction

On the Natural History

of

Destruction

W. G. SEBALD

Translated by Anthea Bell

THE MODERN LIBRARY / NEW YORK

This work was originally published in German by Hanser as
Luftkrieg und Literatur in 1999 and in slightly different form.
Copyright © 1999 by W. G. Sebald. English translation
published by arrangement with Hamish Hamilton,
a publishing division of Penguin Books Ltd.

Grateful acknowledgment is made to Indiana University Press for
permission to reprint excerpts from *At the Mind's Limits* by Jean
Améry, translated by Sidney Rosenfeld and Stella P. Rosenfeld.
Translation copyright © 1980 by Indiana University Press.
Reprinted by permission of Indiana University Press.

LIBRARY OF CONGRESS CATALOGING-IN-PUBLICATION DATA
Sebald, Winfried Georg, 1944–2001
[Luftkrieg und Literatur. English]
On the natural history of destruction: with essays on Alfred Andersch,
Jean Améry, and Peter Weiss / W. G. Sebald; translated by Anthea Bell.
p.   cm.
ISBN 978-0-375-75657-3
1. World War, 1939–1945—Literature and the war.   2. German
literature—20th century—History and criticism.   3. Bombing,
Aerial—Germany.   4. World War, 1939–1945—Destruction
and pillage—Germany.   I. Title.
PT405 .S4313 2003   833'.91409358—dc21   2002075187

Modern Library website address: www.modernlibrary.com
Printed in the United States of America

Book design by Casey Hampton

Contents

Foreword

THE LECTURES ON LITERATURE AND THE AIR raids of the Second World War in this volume are not printed exactly as I delivered them in the late autumn of 1997. The idea behind the first lecture came from Carl Seelig's account of an excursion he made in the summer of 1943 with Robert Walser, then a patient in a mental hospital, on the very day before the night when the city of Hamburg went up in flames. Seelig's reminiscences, which make no reference at all to this coincidence, gave me a clearer view of the perspective from which I myself look back on the terrible events of those years. Born in a village in the Allgäu Alps in May 1944, I am one of those who remained almost untouched by the catastrophe then unfolding in the German Reich. In my first Zürich lecture

I tried to show, through passages of some length taken from my own literary works, that this catastrophe had nonetheless left its mark on my mind. On that occasion, such an approach could be justified, since the ostensible subject of my lectures was poetics. In the version presented here, however, extensive self-quotation would be inappropriate. I have therefore merely used parts of my first lecture in a postscript, which also deals with the reactions to what I said in Zürich and the correspondence that I subsequently received. Much of the response was rather bizarre in character. However, the inadequate and inhibited nature of the letters and other writings sent to me showed, in itself, that the sense of unparalleled national humiliation felt by millions in the last years of the war had never really found verbal expression, and that those directly affected by the experience neither shared it with each other nor passed it on to the next generation. The recurrent complaint that no one, to the present day, has written the great German epic of the wartime and postwar periods is not unconnected with this failure (which in some ways is entirely understandable), given the force of the absolute uncertainty that emerged from our order-loving minds. In spite of strenuous efforts to come to terms with the past, as people like to put it, it seems to me that we Germans today are a nation strikingly blind to history and lacking in tradition. We do not feel any passionate interest in our earlier way of life and the specific features of our own civilization, of the kind universally perceptible, for instance, in the culture of the British Isles. And when we turn to take a retrospective view, particularly of the years 1930 to 1950, we are always looking and looking away at the same time. As a result, the works produced by German authors after the war are often marked by a half-consciousness or false consciousness designed to consolidate the extremely precarious position of those writers in a society that was morally almost entirely discredited. To the overwhelming majority of the writers who stayed on in Germany under the Third Reich, the redefinition of their idea of themselves after 1945 was a more urgent business than depiction of the real conditions surrounding them. The case of Alfred Andersch was a good example of the unfortunate consequences in literary practice, and for that reason the essay on him which I published in *Lettre* a few years ago is reprinted here, after the lectures on air war and literature. At the time it earned me several sharp reprimands from people unwilling to see that, as the apparently inexorable power of the Fascist regime was deployed, a basic stance of opposition and a lively intelligence, characteristics undoubtedly typical of Andersch, could easily turn into more or less deliberate attempts to conform, and that later a man in the public eye, like Andersch, would therefore have to adjust his presentation of his career, through tactful omissions and other revisions. In my view, such a preoccupation with retrospective improvement of the self-image they wished to hand down was one of the main reasons for the inability of a whole generation of German authors to describe what they had seen, and to convey it to our minds.

Translator's note: This is the foreword as written for the German edition of the book published by Hanser in 1999. The English edition, it will be seen, also includes essays on Jean Améry and Peter Weiss, which were not part of the original German publication. I have no doubt that if he had lived to see the final text of the full translation—he had already approved the whole of the earlier part—W. G. Sebald would have revised or added to the foreword in order to include mention of those two authors.

Air War and Literature

Zürich Lectures

THE TRICK OF ELIMINATION IS
EVERY EXPERT'S DEFENSIVE REFLEX.

Stanisław Lem, Imaginary Magnitude

TODAY IT IS HARD TO FORM AN EVEN PARTLY adequate idea of the extent of the devastation suffered by the cities of Germany in the last years of the Second World War, still harder to think about the horrors involved in that devastation. It is true that the strategic bombing surveys published by the Allies, together with the records of the Federal German Statistics Office and other official sources, show that the Royal Air Force alone dropped a million tons of bombs on enemy territory; it is true that of the 131 towns and cities attacked, some only once and some repeatedly, many were almost entirely flattened, that about 600,000 German civilians fell victim to the air raids, and that three and a half million homes were destroyed, while at the end of the war seven and a half million people were left homeless, and there were 31.1 cubic meters of rubble for every person in Cologne and 42.8 cubic meters for every inhabitant of Dresden—but we do not grasp what it all actually meant.[1] The destruction, on a scale without historical precedent, entered the annals of the nation, as it set about rebuilding itself, only in the form of vague generalizations. It seems to have left scarcely a trace of pain behind in the collective consciousness, it has been largely obliterated from the retrospective understanding of those affected, and it never played any appreciable part in the discussion of the internal constitution of our country. As Alexander Kluge later confirmed, it never became an experience capable of public decipherment.[2] This is highly paradoxical in view of the large numbers of people exposed to the campaign day after day, month after month, year after year, and the length of time—well into the postwar period—during which they still faced its real consequences, which might have been expected to stifle any positive attitude to life. Despite the enormous efforts whereby some kind of practicable modus vivendi was restored after every attack, even after 1950 wooden crosses still stood on the piles of rubble in towns like Pforzheim, which lost almost one-third of its 60,000 inhabitants in a single raid on the night of February 22, 1945, and no doubt the appalling smells which, as Janet Flanner wrote in March 1947, were released from the yawning cellars of Warsaw by the first

warm spring weather pervaded the German cities, too, in the immediate postwar period.[3] But these things obviously did not register on the sensory experience of the survivors still living on the scene of the catastrophe. People walked "down the street and past the dreadful ruins," wrote Alfred Döblin in 1945, after returning from his American exile to southwest Germany, "as if nothing had happened, and . . . the town had always looked like that."[4] The reverse side of such apathy was the declaration of a new beginning, the unquestioning heroism with which people immediately set about the task of clearance and reorganization. A booklet devoted to the city of Worms in 1945–1955 says that "the hour called for upright men of impeccable conduct and aims, almost all of whom would be in the front line of reconstruction for years to come."[5] This booklet, written by one Willi Ruppert for the munic-

Kämmererstraße: Kein Haus überstand das Inferno

ipal authorities, included many photographs, including the two pictures of the Kämmererstrasse printed here. They make it look as if the image of total destruction was not the horrifying end of a collective aberration, but something more like the first stage of a brave new world. Writing of a conversation with the directors of I. G. Farben in Frankfurt in April 1945, Robert Thomas Pell records the amazement with which he heard Germans stating their intention of rebuilding their country to be "greater and stronger than ever before"—in a tone in which self-pity, groveling self-justification, a sense of injured innocence, and defiance were curiously intermingled.[6] Nor did they subsequently fail to carry out that intention, as witness the postcards that travelers in Germany can buy today at the newsstands of Frankfurt am Main.

Schöner und breiter erstand sie wieder

From the outset, the now legendary and in some respects genuinely admirable reconstruction of the country after the devastation wrought by Germany's wartime enemies, a reconstruction tantamount to a second liquidation in successive phases of the nation's own past history, prohibited any look backward. It did so through the sheer amount of labor required and the creation of a new, faceless reality, pointing the population exclusively towards the future and enjoining on it silence about the past. German accounts of the time, which is scarcely a generation ago, are so few and far between that Hans Magnus Enzensberger's collection *Europa in Trümmern* ("Europe in Ruins"), published in 1990, consists predominantly of pieces by foreign journalists and writers making observations that until then had been almost completely ignored in

Frankfurt am Main   *Blick zum Römer 1947*

FRANKFURT – GESTERN + HEUTE

Blick zum Römer 1997

Germany. The few accounts originally written in German are by former exiles or other outsiders, such as Max Frisch. Those who had stayed in Germany and, like Walter von Molo and Frank Thiess in the deplorable controversy over Thomas Mann, were fond of saying that while others were comfortably ensconced in America they themselves had not left their homeland in its hour of need, refrained entirely from commenting on the process and outcome of destruction, probably not least for fear that accurate descriptions might get them into trouble with the occupying forces. Contrary to popular opinion, this shortage of contemporary accounts was not compensated for in postwar German literature which, as it followed a deliberate program of renewal after 1947, might have been expected to cast some light on the real state of affairs. Whilst the old guard of so-called internal emigrants claimed to have been engaged in passive resistance, invoking, as Enzensberger notes, vague notions of freedom and the humanist inheritance of the West in endless and prolix abstractions,[7] the younger generation of writers who had just returned home were so intent on their own wartime experiences, described in a style constantly lapsing into maudlin sentimentality, that they hardly seemed to notice the horrors which, at that time, surrounded them on all sides. Even the frequently cited "literature of the ruins," of its nature presupposing an unerring sense of reality and chiefly concerned, as Heinrich Böll acknowledged, with "what we found when we came home,"[8] proves on closer inspection to be an instrument already tuned to individual and collective amnesia, and probably influenced by preconscious self-censorship—a means of obscuring a world that could no longer be presented in comprehensible terms. There was a tacit agreement, equally binding on everyone, that the true state of material and moral ruin in which the country found itself was not to be described. The darkest aspects of the final act of destruction, as experienced by the great majority of the German population, remained under a kind of taboo like a shameful family secret, a secret that perhaps could not even be privately acknowledged. Of all the literary works written at the end of the 1940s, probably only Heinrich Böll's *Der Engel schwieg* ("The Angel Was Silent") gives some idea of the depths of horror then threatening to overwhelm any who really looked at the ruins around them.[9] Reading it, one is immediately aware that this of all novels, a tale which seems marked by irremediable gloom, was more than readers of the time could be expected to take, as Böll's publishers and probably Böll himself thought. As a result it was not published until 1992, almost fifty years later. Indeed, the seventeenth chapter, relating the death throes of Frau Gompertz, is so unremittingly somber that even today it makes painful reading. The dark, stickily clotting blood described in these pages as it pours from the dying woman's mouth in floods and spasms, spreading over her chest, staining the sheets, dripping over the edge of the bed to the floor and forming a glutinous puddle—inky and, as Böll is at pains to emphasize, intensely black-hued blood—symbolizes the despair that militates against the will to survive, the bleak depression that refuses to lift and to which the Germans might have been expected to succumb in view of such a horrific end. Apart from Heinrich Böll, only a few authors—Hermann Kasack, Hans Erich Nossack, Arno Schmidt, and Peter de Mendelssohn—ventured to break the taboo on any mention of the inward and outward destruction, and as we shall see, they generally did so rather equivocally. Even in later years, when local and amateur war historians began documenting the fall of the German cities, their studies did not alter the fact that the images of this horrifying chapter of our history have never really crossed the threshold of the national consciousness. Those compilations, as a rule published by more or less obscure firms—Hans Brunswig's *Feuersturm über Hamburg* ("Firestorm over Hamburg"), for instance, was issued in 1978 by Motorbuch-Verlag of Stuttgart—often seemed curiously untouched by the subject of their research, and served primarily to sanitize or eliminate a kind of knowledge incompatible with any sense of normality. They did not try to provide a clearer understanding of the extraordinary faculty for self-anesthesia shown by a community that seemed to have emerged from a war of annihilation without any signs of psychological impairment. The almost entire absence of profound disturbance to the inner life of the nation suggests that the new Federal German society relegated the experiences of its own prehistory to the back of its mind and developed an almost perfectly functioning mechanism of repression, one which allowed it to recognize the fact of its own rise from total degradation while disengaging entirely from its stock of emotions, if not actually chalking up as another item to its credit its success in overcoming all tribulations without showing any sign of weakness. Enzensberger points out that it is impossible to understand "the mysterious energy of the Germans . . . if we refuse to realize that they have made a virtue of their deficiencies. Insensibility," he adds, "was the condition of their success."[10] The prerequisites of the German economic miracle were not only the enormous sums invested in the country under the Marshall Plan, the outbreak of the Cold War, and the scrapping of outdated industrial complexes—an operation performed with brutal efficiency by the bomber squadrons—but also something less often acknowledged: the unquestioning work ethic learned in a totalitarian society, the logistical capacity for improvisation shown by an economy under constant threat, experience in the use of "foreign labor forces," and the lifting of the heavy burden of history that went up in flames between 1942 and 1945 along with the centuries-old buildings accommodating homes and businesses in Nuremberg and Cologne, in Frankfurt, Aachen,

Brunswick, and Würzburg, a historical burden ultimately regretted by only a few. And in addition to these more or less identifiable factors in the genesis of the economic miracle, there was also a purely immaterial catalyst: the stream of psychic energy that has not dried up to this day, and which has its source in the well-kept secret of the corpses built into the foundations of our state, a secret that bound all Germans together in the postwar years, and indeed still binds them, more closely than any positive goal such as the realization of democracy ever could. Perhaps we ought to remind ourselves of that context now, when the project of creating a greater Europe, a project that has already failed twice, is entering a new phase, and the sphere of influence of the Deutschmark—history has a way of repeating itself—seems to extend almost precisely to the confines of the area occupied by the Wehrmacht in the year 1941.

The plan for an all-out bombing campaign, which had been supported by groups within the Royal Air Force since 1940, came into effect in February 1942, with the deployment of huge quantities of personnel and war matériel. As far as I know, the question of whether and how it could be strategically or morally justified was never the subject of open debate in Germany after 1945, no doubt mainly because a nation which had murdered and worked to death millions of people in its camps could hardly call on the victorious powers to explain the military and political logic that dictated the destruction of the German cities. It is also possible, as sources like Hans Erich Nossack's account of the destruction of Hamburg indicate, that quite a number of those affected by the air raids, despite their grim but impotent fury in the face of such obvious madness, regarded the great firestorms as a just punishment, even an act of retribution on the part of a higher power with which there could be no dispute. Apart from the reports of the Nazi press and the Reich broadcasting service, which always spoke in the same tone of sadistic terrorist attacks and barbaric gangsters of the air, protests against the long campaign of destruction conducted by the Allies seem to have been few and far between. According to several accounts, the Germans faced the catastrophe that was taking place with silent fascination. "This was not the time," wrote Nossack, "to draw such petty distinctions as the difference between friend and foe."[11] But in contrast to the mainly passive reaction of the Germans to the loss of their cities, which they perceived as an inescapable calamity, the program of destruction was vigorously debated from the first in Great Britain. Not only did Lord Salisbury and George Bell, Bishop of Chichester, repeatedly and very forcefully express the opinion, both in the House of Lords and to the general public, that an attacking strategy directed primarily against the civilian population could not be defended morally or by the laws of war, but the military establishment responsible for conducting the campaign was itself split over this new kind of warfare. The continuing ambivalence in the appraisal of the battle of annihilation was even more pronounced after Germany's unconditional surrender. As accounts and pictures of the effects of area bombing began appearing in England, there was a growing sense of revulsion against damage that had been, so to speak, indiscriminately inflicted. "In the safety of peace," writes Max Hastings, "the bombers' part in the war was one that many politicians and civilians would prefer to forget."[12] Retrospective historical accounts did not clear up the ethical dilemma either. Feuds between various factions were continued in memoirs, and the verdict of historians trying to maintain an objective balance swings between admiration for the organization of such a mighty enterprise, and criticism of the futility and atrocity of an operation mercilessly carried through to the end against the dictates of good sense.

The origin of the area-bombing strategy lay in the extremely marginal position of Great Britain in 1941. Germany was at the height of its power; its armies had conquered the entire continent of Europe and were about to advance farther into Africa and Asia; and the British were simply left to their insular fate without any real chance of intervening in the action. With this prospect before him, Churchill wrote to Lord Beaverbrook that there was only one way to force Hitler back to confrontation, "and that is an absolutely devastating exterminating attack by very heavy bombers from this country upon the Nazi homeland."[13] Admittedly the prerequisites for such an operation were far from present at the time. The basis of production was inadequate; there were not enough airfields; and training programs for bomber crews were in short supply, as were effective explosives, new navigational systems, and almost any kind of useful experience. The bizarre projects being seriously pursued in the early 1940s show how desperate the situation was as a whole. For instance, a plan was under consideration for dropping iron stake-tips over arable land to sabotage the harvest, and Max Perutz, a glaciologist in exile, was busy carrying out experiments for Project Habbakuk, with the idea of producing a gigantic and unsinkable aircraft carrier made of a kind of artificially reinforced ice called pykrete. Scarcely less fantastic were the attempts of the time to construct a defense network of invisible rays, or the complicated calculations being carried out at Birmingham University by Rudolf Peierls and Otto Frisch which brought the building of an atomic bomb into the realm of feasibility. Against a background of ideas verging on the improbable like these, it is not surprising that the far more easily comprehensible strategy of area bombing finally got the go-ahead. It was a strategy which, notwithstanding the small degree of accuracy in hitting a target, allowed a kind of mobile front line to be drawn the length and breadth of enemy territory, and it was sanctioned by the governmental decision of February 1942 "to destroy the morale of the enemy civilian population and, in particular, of the industrial workers."[14]

This directive did not, as is frequently claimed, spring from a wish to bring the war to a speedy conclusion by the massive deployment of bombers; it was the only way of intervening in the war at all. The criticism later leveled at the ruthless pursuit of such a program of destruction (partly in view of the Allies' own casualties) concentrated chiefly on the fact that it was sustained even when selective attacks could be made from the air, with far greater precision, on targets like factories making ball-bearings, oil and fuel installations, railway junctions, and the main transport arteries—operations which, as Albert Speer commented in his memoirs, would very soon have paralyzed the entire system of production.[15] Critics of the bombing offensive also pointed out that, even in the spring of 1944, it was emerging that despite incessant air raids the morale of the German population was obviously unbroken, while industrial production was impaired only marginally at best, and the end of the war had not come a day closer. I believe that if, nonetheless, the strategic aims of the offensive were not modified, and the bomber crews, many of them boys who had only just left school, were still exposed to a game of Russian roulette costing sixty out of a hundred of them their lives, it was for reasons largely ignored in the official histories. One was that an enterprise of the material and organizational dimensions of the bombing offensive, which by A.J.P. Taylor's estimate swallowed up one-third of the entire British production of war matériel,[16] had such a momentum of its own that short-term corrections in course and restrictions were more or less ruled out, especially when, after three years of the intensive expansion of factories and production plants, that enterprise had reached the peak of its development—in other words, its maximum destructive capacity. Once the matériel was manufactured, simply letting the aircraft and their valuable freight stand idle on the airfields of eastern England ran counter to any healthy economic instinct. And a conclusive factor in deciding to continue the offensive was probably the propaganda value, essential for bolstering British morale, of the daily reports of systematic destruction in British newspapers at a time when all other contact with the enemy on the continent of Europe had been cut off. For these reasons there can hardly have been any question of sacking Sir Arthur Harris, commander-in-chief of Bomber Command, who still inflexibly supported his strategy even when it was obviously not working. Some commentators also claim "that 'Bomber' Harris had managed to secure a peculiar hold over the otherwise domineering, intrusive Churchill,"[17] for although on various occasions the Prime

Minister expressed certain scruples about the horrifying bombardment of defenseless cities he consoled himself— obviously under the influence of Harris and his dismissal of any arguments against his policy—with the idea that there was now, as he put it, a higher poetic justice at work and "that those who have loosed these horrors upon mankind will now in their homes and persons feel the shattering strokes of just retribution."[18] In fact, there is much to suggest that in Harris a man had risen to the head of Bomber Command who, according to Solly Zuckerman, liked destruction for its own sake,[19] and was thus in perfect sympathy with the innermost principle of every war, which is to aim for as wholesale an annihilation of the enemy with his dwellings, his history, and his natural environment as can possibly be achieved. Elias Canetti has linked the fascination of power in its purest form to the growing number of its accumulated victims. In line with this idea, Sir Arthur Harris's position was unassailable *because* of his unlimited interest in destruction. His plan for successive devastating strikes, which he followed uncompromisingly to the end, was overwhelmingly simple in its logic, and by comparison any real strategic alternatives such as disabling the fuel supply were bound to look like mere diversionary tactics. The war in the air was war pure and undisguised. Its continuation in the face of all reason suggests that, as Elaine Scarry has put it in her extremely perspicacious book *The Body in Pain,* the victims of war are not sacrifices made as the means to an end of any kind, but in the most precise sense are both the means and the end in themselves.[20]

The majority of the available sources for the destruction of the German cities—sources widely dispersed, of different kinds, and usually fragmentary—are notable for a curious blindness to experience, the result of extremely narrow, biased, or skewed perspectives. The first live report of a raid on Berlin, for instance, transmitted by the BBC Home Service, is rather a disappointment to anyone expecting it to provide insight into the event from some superior viewpoint. Since despite the ever-present danger very little capable of description at all happened on these night flights, the reporter (Wynford Vaughan-Thomas) had to manage with a minimum of facts. Only the emotion he injects into his voice now and then averts an impression of tedium. We hear the heavy Lancaster bombers take off at nightfall; soon afterwards, they are flying out over the North Sea, with the white breakers on the coastline below them. "Now, right before us," comments Vaughan-Thomas, with an audible tremor in his voice, "lies darkness and Germany." The duration of the flight is of course much abbreviated in the recording, but during the aircraft's approach to the first batteries of lights on the Kammhuber Line listeners are introduced to the crew: Scottie the flight engineer, who used to be a cinema pro-

jectionist in Glasgow before the war; Sparky the bom-
bardier; Connolly, "the navigator, an Aussie from Brisbane";
"the mid-upper gunner, who was in advertising before the
war, and the rear gunner, a Sussex farmer." The skipper
remains anonymous. "We are now well out over the sea
and looking out all the time towards the enemy coast."
Various observations and technical instructions are ex-
changed. Now and then the drone of the big engines can
be heard. Then events follow one another in rapid succes-
sion as the plane approaches the city. Searchlights, inter-
spersed with salvos of light from the flak, reach out to the
planes; one plane is shot down. Vaughan-Thomas tries to
find appropriate ways of emphasizing the dramatic cli-
max; he speaks of a "wall of searchlights, in hundreds, in
cones and clusters. It's a wall of light with very few breaks
and behind that wall is a pool of fiercer light, glowing red
and green and blue, and over that pool myriads of flares
hanging in the sky. That's the city itself! . . . It's going to
be quite soundless," continues Vaughan-Thomas, "the roar
of our aircraft is drowning everything else. We are running straight into the most gigantic display of soundless
fireworks in the world, and here we go to drop our bombs
on Berlin." But after this prelude, there is not really anything more; everything happens much too fast. The aircraft is already flying out of the target area. The crew
members release their tension in sudden loquacity. "Not
too much nattering," the skipper tells them. "By God, that

looks like a bloody good show," says one. "Best I've ever seen," adds another. And then, after some time, a third voice, rather quieter, speaking with something like awe: "Look at that fire! Oh boy!"[21]

There were many such great fires at the time. I once heard a former aircraft gunner say that from his place in his glazed turret at the rear of the plane, he could still see the burning city of Cologne even when they were on their way out again over the Dutch coast; it was a fiery speck in the darkness, like the tail of a motionless comet. It was certainly possible to see Nuremberg in flames from Erlangen and Forchheim, and the fiery glow over Mannheim and Ludwigshafen was visible from the heights around Heidelberg. The Prince of Hesse stood on the outskirts of his park on the night of September 11, 1944, and looked towards Darmstadt, fifteen kilometers away: "The light grew and grew until the whole of the southern sky was glowing, shot through with red and yellow."[22] A prisoner in the Kleine Festung in Theresienstadt remembers clearly seeing, from his cell window, the glowing red reflection above the burning city of Dresden seventy kilometers away, and hearing the hollow thud of the bombs, like hundredweight sacks being thrown into a cellar quite close to him.[23] Friedrich Reck, who shortly before the end of the war was sent to Dachau by the Fascists for uttering subversive opinions, and died there of typhus, noted in his diary—the value of which as genuine contemporary evidence can hardly be overestimated—that during the air raid on Munich in July 1944 the ground shook and pressure waves broke windows as far away as the Chiemgau area.[24] While these were the unmistakable signs of catastrophe engulfing the whole country, it was not always easy to get a more detailed picture of the manner and extent of the destruction. The need to know was at odds with a desire to close down the senses. On the one hand, large quantities of disinformation were circulating; on the other, there were true stories that exceeded anyone's capacity to grasp them. There were said to be 200,000 dead in Hamburg. Reck writes that he cannot believe all he hears, for he has been told a good deal about "the severely confused state of mind of these refugees from Hamburg . . . their amnesia, the way they wander around clad only in pajamas, just as they were when they fled from their collapsing homes."[25] Nossack gives a similar account. "In the first few days you could get no definite information. The details of the stories were never accurate."[26] Obviously, in the shock of what these people had experienced, their ability to remember was partly suspended, or else, in compensation, it worked to an arbitrary pattern. Those who had escaped the catastrophe were unreliable and partly blinded witnesses. Alexander Kluge's account "The Air Raid on Halberstadt on 8 April 1945," which was not in fact written until around 1970 but which finally raises the question of the effects of the so-called moral bombing, quotes an American military psychologist who gleaned the impression after the war, from conversations with survivors in Halberstadt, that "the population, although obviously showing an innate wish to tell its own story, [had] lost the psychic power of accurate memory, particularly within the confines of the ruined city."[27] Even if this opinion, allegedly that of a real person, is one of Kluge's famous pseudo-documentary devices, it is certainly accurate in identifying the syndrome, for the accounts of those who escaped with nothing but their lives do generally have something discontinuous about them, a curiously erratic quality so much at variance with authentic recollection that it easily suggests rumor-mongering and invention. However, the rather unreal effect of the eyewitness reports also derives from the clichés to which they often resorted. The reality of total destruction, incomprehensible in its extremity, pales when described in such stereotypical phrases as "a prey to the flames," "that fateful night," "all hell was let loose," "we were staring into the inferno," "the dreadful fate of the cities of Germany," and so on and so forth. Their function is to cover up and neutralize experiences beyond our ability to comprehend. The phrase "On that dreadful day when our beautiful city was razed to the ground," which Kluge's American investigator encountered in Frankfurt and Fürth, in Wuppertal, Würzburg and Halberstadt alike, is really no more than a gesture sketched to banish memory.[28] Even Victor Klemperer's diary entry on the fall of Dresden remains within the bounds of verbal convention.[29] From what we now know about the ruin of this city it seems unlikely that anyone who then stood on the Brühl Terrace, with the air full of flying sparks, and saw the conflagration all around can have escaped with an undisturbed mind. The apparently unimpaired ability—shown in most of the eyewitness reports—of everyday language to go on functioning as usual raises doubts of the authenticity of the experiences they record. The death by fire within a few hours of an entire city, with all its buildings and its trees, its inhabitants, its domestic pets, its fixtures and fittings of every kind, must inevitably have led to overload, to paralysis of the capacity to think and feel in those who succeeded in escaping. The accounts of individual eyewitnesses, therefore, are of only qualified value, and need to be supplemented by what a synoptic and artificial view reveals.

In the summer of 1943, during a long heat wave, the RAF, supported by the U.S. Eighth Army Air Force, flew a series of raids on Hamburg. The aim of Operation Gomorrah, as it was called, was to destroy the city and reduce it as completely as possible to ashes. In a raid early in the morning of July 27, beginning at one A.M., ten thousand tons of high-explosive and incendiary bombs were dropped on the densely populated residential area east of the Elbe, comprising the districts of Hammerbrook, Hamm-Nord and Hamm-Süd, Billwerder Ausschlag and parts of St. Georg, Eilbek, Barmbek, and Wandsbek. A now familiar sequence of events occurred: first all the doors and windows were torn from their frames and smashed by high-explosive bombs weighing four thousand pounds, then the attic floors of the buildings were ignited by lightweight incendiary mixtures, and at the same time firebombs weighing up to fifteen kilograms fell into the lower stories. Within a few minutes, huge fires were burning all over the target area, which covered some twenty square kilometers, and they merged so rapidly that only a quarter of an hour after the first bombs had dropped the whole airspace was a sea of flames as far as the eye could see. Another five minutes later, at one-twenty A.M., a firestorm of an intensity that no one would ever before have thought possible arose. The fire, now rising two thousand meters into the sky, snatched oxygen to itself so violently that the air currents reached hurricane force, resonating like mighty organs with all their stops pulled out at once. The fire burned like this for three hours. At its height, the storm lifted gables and roofs from buildings, flung rafters and entire advertising billboards through the air, tore trees from the ground, and drove human beings before it like living torches. Behind collapsing façades, the flames shot up as high as houses, rolled like a tidal wave through the streets at a speed of over a hundred and fifty kilometers an hour, spun across open squares in strange rhythms like rolling cylinders of fire. The water in some of the canals was ablaze. The glass in the tram car windows melted; stocks of sugar boiled in the bakery cellars. Those who had fled from their air-raid shelters sank, with grotesque contortions, in the thick bubbles thrown up by the melting asphalt. No one knows for certain how many lost their lives that night, or how many went mad before they died. When day broke, the summer dawn could not penetrate the leaden gloom above the city. The smoke had risen to a height of eight thousand meters, where it spread like a vast, anvil-shaped cumulonimbus cloud. A wavering heat, which the bomber pilots said they had felt through the sides of their planes, continued to rise from the smoking, glowing mounds of stone. Residential districts so large that their total street length amounted to two hundred

kilometers were utterly destroyed. Horribly disfigured corpses lay everywhere. Bluish little phosphorous flames still flickered around many of them; others had been roasted brown or purple and reduced to a third of their normal size. They lay doubled up in pools of their own melted fat, which had sometimes already congealed. The central death zone was declared off-limits in the next few days. When punishment labor gangs and camp inmates could begin clearing it in August, after the rubble had cooled down, they found people still sitting at tables or up against walls where they had been overcome by monoxide gas. Elsewhere, clumps of flesh and bone or whole heaps of bodies had cooked in the water gushing from bursting boilers. Other victims had been so badly charred and re-duced to ashes by the heat, which had risen to a thousand degrees or more, that the remains of families consisting of several people could be carried away in a single laundry basket.

The exodus of survivors from Hamburg had begun on the night of the air raid itself. It started, as Nossack writes, with "constant movement in all the neighboring streets . . . going no one knew where."[30] The refugees, numbering one and a quarter million, dispersed all over the Reich, as far as its outer borders. Under his diary entry for August 20, 1943, in the passage already quoted above, Friedrich Reck describes a group of forty to fifty such refugees trying to force their way into a train at a station in Upper Bavaria. As they do so, a cardboard suitcase "falls on the platform, bursts open and spills its contents. Toys, a manicure case, singed underwear. And last of all, the roasted corpse of a child, shrunk like a mummy, which its half-deranged mother has been carrying about with her, the relic of a past that was still intact a few days ago."[31] It is hard to imagine that Reck can have invented this dreadful scene. All over Germany, one way or another, news of the horrors of the destruction of Hamburg must have been spread by distraught refugees vacillating between a hysterical will to survive and leaden apathy. Reck's diary at least makes it clear that in spite of the news blackout suppressing all detailed information, it was not impossible to know how horribly the cities of Germany were being destroyed. A year later Reck describes tens of thousands camping out around the Maximilian-platz after the latest major raid on Munich. He writes: "On the nearby main road an endless stream of refugees [is moving], frail old women with bundles containing their last possessions carried on sticks over their backs. Poor homeless people with burnt clothing, their eyes reflecting the horror of the firestorm, the explosions blowing everything to bits, burial in the rubble or the ignominy of suffocating in a cellar."[32] The remarkable aspect of such accounts is their rarity. Indeed, it seems that no German writer, with the sole exception of Nossack, was ready or able to put any concrete facts down on paper about the progress and repercussions of this gigantic, long-term campaign of destruction. It was the same when the war was over. The quasi-natural reflex, engendered by feelings of shame and a wish to defy the victors, was to keep quiet and look the other way. Stig Dagerman, reporting from Germany in the autumn of 1946 for the Swedish newspaper *Expressen,* writes from Hamburg that on a train going at normal speed it took him a quarter of an hour to travel through the lunar landscape between Hasselbrook and Landwehr, and in all that vast wilderness, perhaps the most horrifying expanse of ruins in the whole of Europe, he did not see a single living soul. The train, writes Dagerman, was crammed full, like all trains in Germany, but no one looked out of the windows, and he was identified as a foreigner himself *because* he looked out.[33]

Janet Flanner, writing for *The New Yorker,* made similar

observations in Cologne, which, as she said in one of her reports, lay "by its riverbanks . . . recumbent, without beauty, shapeless in the rubble and loneliness of complete physical defeat. Through its clogged streets," the passage continues, "trickles what is left of its life, a dwindled population in black and with bundles—the silent German people appropriate to the silent city."[34] That silence, that reserve, that instinctive looking away are the reasons why we know so little of what the Germans thought and observed in the five years between 1942 and 1947. The ruins where they lived were the terra incognita of the war. Solly Zuckerman may have had a premonition of this deficiency. Like everyone who was directly involved in discussion of the most efficient attacking strategy, and who thus had a certain professional interest in the effects of area bombing, he visited the ravaged city of Cologne at the earliest possible opportunity. On his return to London he still felt overwhelmed by what he had seen, and he agreed to write a report for Cyril Connolly, then editor of the journal *Horizon,* to be entitled "On the Natural History of Destruction." In his autobiography, written decades later, Lord Zuckerman mentions that nothing came of this project. "My first view of Cologne," he says, "cried out for a more eloquent piece than I could ever have written."[35] When I questioned Lord Zuckerman on the subject in the 1980s, he could no longer remember in detail what he had wanted to say at the time. All that remained in his mind was the image of the blackened cathedral rising from the stony desert around it, and the memory of a severed finger that he had found on a heap of rubble.

II

HOW OUGHT SUCH A NATURAL HISTORY OF destruction to begin? With a summary of the technical, organizational, and political prerequisites for carrying out large-scale air raids? With a scientific account of the previously unknown phenomenon of the firestorms? With a pathographical record of typical modes of death, or with behaviorist studies of the instincts of flight and homecoming? Nossack writes that after the raids on Hamburg there were no conduits available for the great tide of people that "silently and inexorably deluged everything," carrying disquiet along little rivulets and into the most remote villages. No sooner did the refugees find accommodation somewhere, Nossack continues, than they set off again, either traveling farther or trying to get back to Hamburg, "whether to salvage something, or to look for relations," or for those dark reasons that compel a murderer to revisit the scene of the crime.[36] In any case, a countless crowd of people was daily on the move. Later, Heinrich Böll suggested that such experiences of collective uprooting are at the origin of the German craving for travel: a sense of being unable to stay anywhere, a constant need to be somewhere else.[37] In terms of social conditioning, this would make the ebb and flow of the population bombed out of their homes rather like a rehearsal for initiation into the mobile society that would form in the decades after the catastrophe. Under the auspices of that society, chronic restlessness became a cardinal virtue.

Apart from the distraught behavior of the people themselves, the most striking change in the natural order of the cities during the weeks after a devastating raid was undoubtedly the sudden and alarming increase in the parasitical creatures thriving on the unburied bodies. The conspicuous sparsity of observations and comments on this phenomenon can be explained as the tacit imposition of a taboo, very understandable if one remembers that the Germans, who had proposed to cleanse and sanitize all Europe, now had to contend with a rising fear that they themselves were the rat people. Böll's novel that lay so long unpublished contains a passage in which he describes a rat among the ruins making its way from a mound of rubble to the street, sniffing the air, and there is a well-known story by Wolfgang Borchert in which a boy keeps watch by the body of his brother, who is buried under the rubble; the watcher's horror of the rats is banished by the assurance that they sleep at night. Otherwise, so far as I can see, the only reference to the subject in the literature of that time is a single passage by Nossack about the convicts in their striped uniforms who were called in to clear away "the remains of what had once been human beings," and could reach the corpses in the air raid shelters of the death zone only with flamethrowers, so densely did the flies swarm around them, and so thick were the floors and steps of the cellars with slippery finger-length maggots. "Rats and flies ruled the city. The rats, bold and fat, frolicked in the streets, but even more disgusting were the flies, huge and iridescent green, flies such as had never been seen before. They swarmed in great clusters on the roads, settled in heaps to copulate on ruined walls, and basked, weary and satiated, on the splinters of the windowpanes. When they could no longer fly they crawled after us through the tiniest of cracks, and their buzzing and whirring was the first thing we heard on waking. It went on until October."[38] This image of the multiplication of species that are usually suppressed in every possible way is a rare documentary record of life in a ravaged city. While the majority of the survivors may have been spared direct confrontation with the most repulsive fauna of the rubble, they were pursued everywhere by the flies at least, not to mention the "stench . . . of rotting and decay" which, as Nossack writes, "lay over the city."[39] There are almost no records of those who succumbed to the sheer nausea of existence during the weeks and months after the destruction, but Hans, for one, the protagonist of *Der Engel schwieg,* feels horror at the idea of having to resume life again, and nothing seems to him more natural than simply to give up, "climb down the stairs and go into the night."[40] Decades later, it is still characteristic of many of Böll's central characters that they lack any real will to live. This deficiency, clinging to them like a stigma in the new world of success, is the legacy of an existence among the ruins that was felt to be shameful. Air Commodore E. J. Kingston-McCloughry, commenting on the terrible and deeply disturbing sight of the apparently aimless wanderings of millions of homeless people amidst this monstrous destruction, makes it clear how close to extinction many of them really were in the ruined cities at the end of the war. No one knew where the homeless stayed, although lights among the ruins after dark showed where they had moved in.[41] This is the necropolis of a foreign, mysterious people, torn from its civil existence and its history, thrown back to the evolutionary stage of nomadic gatherers. Let us therefore imagine "the charred ruins of the city, a dark and jagged silhouette far away beyond the allotments, towering above the railway embankment,"[42] and in front of them a landscape of low mounds of rubble the color of cement, with great clouds of dry, red-brick dust

drifting over the lifeless surroundings, a single human figure poking about in the detritus,[43] a tram stop in the middle of nowhere, people emerging suddenly and, as Böll
writes, apparently out of nowhere, as if they had sprung
from the gray scree, "invisibly, inaudibly . . . out of this
void . . . ghosts whose path and whose goal could not be
perceived: figures burdened with parcels and sacks, crates
and cartons."[44] Let us go back with them to the city where
they live, down streets where moraines of rubble reach up
to the second floors of the burnt-out façades. We see people who have lit small fires in the open (as if they were in
the jungle, writes Nossack), and are cooking their food or
boiling up their laundry on those fires.[45] We see stovepipes
emerging from the remains of walls, smoke slowly dispers-
ing, an old woman in a head scarf with a coal shovel in her
hand.[46] The Fatherland must have looked something like
that in 1945. Stig Dagerman describes the lives of the cave
dwellers in a city in the Ruhr: the unappetizing meals they
concocted from dirty, wrinkled vegetables and dubious
scraps of meat, the cold and hunger that reigned in those
underground caverns, the evil fumes, the water that always
stood on the cellar floors, the coughing children and their
battered and sodden shoes. Dagerman describes school-
rooms in which the broken windowpanes were replaced by
school slates, and where it was so dark that the children
could not read the textbooks in front of them. In Hamburg,
says Dagerman, he talked to one Herr Schumann, a bank

clerk then in his third year of living underground. The white faces of these people, writes Dagerman, were just like the faces of fish coming up to the surface to snatch a breath of air.[47] Victor Gollancz, who spent a month and a half traveling in the British-occupied zone in the autumn of 1946, mainly in Hamburg, Düsseldorf, and the Ruhr, wrote a series of reports for the British press giving details of the population's poor diet, deficiency symptoms, nutritional edemas, emaciation, skin infections, and the rapid rise in the number of cases of tuberculosis. Like Dagerman, Gollancz speaks of people's profound lethargy, describing it as the most striking characteristic of the contemporary urban population at that time. "People drift about with such lassitude," he writes, "that you are always in danger of running them down when you happen to be in a car."[48] Perhaps the most startling of Gollancz's reports from defeated Germany is his brief piece entitled "This Misery of Boots," about the wretched footwear of the Germans—startling not so much for the text itself as for the photographs that illustrated it when Gollancz's articles came out later in book form. The author, obviously fascinated by the subject, had taken the pictures himself in the autumn of 1946. Photographs like these, making the process of degradation visible in very concrete form, are surely part of a natural history of destruction as Solly Zuckerman envisaged it, and so is the passage from *Der Engel schwieg* in which the narra-

tor comments that you could tell the date of a building's destruction from the plants growing among the ruins. "It was
a question of botany. This heap of rubble was bare, naked,
all rough stones and recently shattered masonry . . . with
not a blade of grass in sight, whereas elsewhere trees were
already growing, pretty little trees springing up in bed-
rooms and kitchens." At the end of the war, some of the
bomb sites of Cologne had already been transformed by the
dense green vegetation growing over them—the roads
made their way through this new landscape like "peaceful
deep-set country lanes."[49] In contrast to the effect of the
catastrophes insidiously creeping up on us today, nature's
ability to regenerate did not seem to have been impaired by
the firestorms. In fact, many trees and bushes, particularly

chestnuts and lilacs, had a second flowering in Hamburg in the autumn of 1943, a few months after the great fire.[50] If the Morgenthau Plan had ever been implemented, how long would it have taken for woodland to cover the mountains of ruins all over the country?*

---

*This was a 1944 proposal by the U.S. Secretary of the Treasury, Henry Morgenthau, calling for the postwar "pastoralization" of Germany by the removal of all its heavy industry.

Instead, and with remarkable speed, social life, that other natural phenomenon, revived. People's ability to forget what they do not want to know, to overlook what is before their eyes, was seldom put to the test better than in Germany at that time. The population decided—out of sheer panic at first—to carry on as if nothing had happened. Kluge's account of the destruction of Halberstadt begins with the story of Frau Schrader, employed at a local cinema, who gets to work with a shovel commandeered from the air raid wardens immediately after the bomb falls, hoping "to clear the rubble away before the two o'clock matinee."[51] Down in the cellar, where she finds various cooked body parts, she clears up by dumping them in the washhouse boiler for the time being. On his return to Hamburg a few days after the air raid, Nossack describes seeing a woman cleaning the windows of a building "that stood alone and undamaged in the middle of the desert of ruins. . . . We thought we were looking at a madwoman," he writes, and continues, "We felt the same when we saw children tidying and raking a front garden. It was so far beyond all comprehension that we told other people about it, as if it were some sort of a marvel. One day we came to a suburb that had not suffered at all. People were sitting out on their balconies drinking coffee. It was like watching a film; it was downright impossible."[52] Nossack's sense of alienation arose from seeing himself confronted, as it must have seemed from the viewpoint of one affected, by a lack of moral sensitivity bordering on inhumanity. You do not expect an insect colony to be transfixed with grief at the destruction of a neighboring anthill, but you do assume a certain degree of empathy in human nature, and to that extent there is indeed something alarmingly absurd and shocking about continuing to drink coffee in the normal way on Hamburg balconies at the end of July 1943, rather like the sight of Grandville's animals, in human dress and armed with cutlery, consuming a fellow creature. On the other hand, keeping up everyday routines regardless of disaster, from the baking of a cake to put on the coffee table to the observance of more elevated cultural rituals, is a tried and trusted method of preserving what is thought of as healthy human reason. The role of music in the evolution and collapse of the German Reich is part of this context. Whenever it seemed advisable to invoke the gravity of the hour a full orchestra was conscripted, and the regime identified itself with the affirmative statement of the symphonic finale. The carpet-bombing of the cities of Germany made no difference. Alexander Kluge remembers a performance of *Aida* broadcast by Radio Roma the night before the raid on Halberstadt. "We sit in my father's bedroom, in front of a brown wooden radio set with an illuminated dial bearing the names of the foreign stations on it, listening to the distorted, secret music coming from far away, with interference, telling some kind of serious story briefly summarized for us by our father in German. Around one A.M. the lovers go to their deaths in the tomb."[53] And on the evening before the devastating raid on Darmstadt, according to one survivor, he "listened on the radio to some songs from the sensuous Rococo world of Strauss's magical music."[54] Nossack, to whom the empty façades of Hamburg look like triumphal arches, Roman ruins, or stage sets for some fantastic opera, gazes down from a mound of rubble on a desert, with only the porch of the convent garden left standing. He had been to a concert there in March. "A blind woman singer performed; she sang 'Die schwere Leidenszeit beginnt nun abermals'—'The time of suffering now begins once more.' Simple and self-assured, she leaned against the harpsichord, and her unseeing eyes looked past those trivialities for which we already feared, past them and perhaps to the place where we now stood, with nothing but a sea of stones around us."[55] The linking of the sacred with the utmost profanity, evoked here through a musical experience, is a device that always proves effective. "A hilly landscape of bricks, human beings buried beneath it, the stars above; the last moving things are the rats. Went to hear *Iphigenie* in the evening," noted Max Frisch in a diary entry written in Berlin.[56] An English observer remembers an operatic performance in the same city just after the cease-fire. "In the midst of such shambles only the Germans," he comments with rather double-edged admiration, "could produce a magnificent full orchestra and a crowded house of music lovers."[57] Who could deny that the audiences of the time, eyes shining as they listened once more to the sound of music rising in the air all over the country, were moved by a sense of gratitude that they had been saved? Yet we may also wonder whether their breasts did not swell with perverse pride to think that no one in human history had ever played such overwhelming tunes or endured such suffering as the Germans. These ideas are recorded in the life story of the German composer Adrian Leverkühn "as told by a friend," the Freising schoolmaster Zeitblom, inspired by his ghostwriter in Santa Barbara, when the city of Dürer and Pirckheimer lay in ashes and nearby Munich was suffering too. "My sympathetic readers and friends, let me go on with my tale. Over Germany destruction thickens. Rats grown fat on corpses housed in the rubble of our cities. . . ."[58] In *Doctor Faustus,* Thomas Mann wrote a comprehensive historical criticism of an art that was increasingly inclined to take an apocalyptic view of the world, at the same time confessing his own involvement. It is likely that few of the readers for whom this novel was originally intended understood him; the lava barely cold under their feet, they were too preoccupied with the reaffirmation of their higher ideals, too anxious to free themselves of any taint. They did not go deeply

into the complex question of the relationship between ethics and aesthetics that tormented Thomas Mann. Yet that question would have been of central importance, as the paucity of literary accounts of the destruction of the German cities suggests.

Besides Heinrich Böll, whose melancholy novel of the ruins *Der Engel schwieg* was withheld from the reading public for over forty years, the only authors who did write about the destruction of the cities and postwar survival in a landscape of ruins were Hermann Kasack, Hans Erich Nossack, and Peter de Mendelssohn. The three of them were linked by this common interest at the time. Kasack and Nossack had been in regular contact since around 1942, when they were working on *Die Stadt hinter dem Strom* ("The City Beyond the River") and *Nekyia* respectively; Mendelssohn, who had been living in exile in England and could scarcely grasp the full extent of the destruction when he first returned to Germany in May 1945, felt—surely on the grounds of this impression— that Kasack's work, which appeared in the spring of 1947, was a highly topical contemporary document. That same summer he wrote an enthusiastic review, tried to find an English publisher for the book, and immediately started translating it himself. In 1948, as a result of his interest in Kasack, he began work on his own novel *Die Kathedrale* ("The Cathedral"), which like the titles by Kasack and Nossack is to be seen as a literary experiment written in the ambience of total destruction. The many tasks that Mendelssohn had to shoulder while he was working for the military government, helping to rebuild the German press, made him shelve the project, and the story, which was first written in English, remained a fragment. It was published, still in fragmentary form and in Mendelssohn's own German version, only in 1983. The key text of this group is undoubtedly *Die Stadt hinter dem Strom,* a work generally considered at the time to be of epoch-making significance, and long regarded as the last word on the insanity of the National Socialist regime. "With a single book," wrote Nossack, "German literature was reinstated at the highest level, literature that had been created here, grown on our ruins."[59] Exactly how Kasack's work of fiction reflected conditions in Germany at the time is, of course, another question, and so is the meaning of the philosophy he extrapolated from those conditions. The city beyond the river in which "life, so to speak, is lived underground"[60] manifests itself as in every way a shattered community. "Only the façades of the buildings in the surrounding streets still stood, so that a sideways glance through the rows of empty windows gave a view of the sky."[61] And it could be argued that the account of the "lifeless life"[62] of the people in this twilight kingdom was also inspired by the real economic and social situation between 1943 and 1947. There are no vehicles anywhere, and pedestrians walk the ruined streets apathetically, "as if they no longer felt the bleak nature of their surroundings. . . . Others could be seen in the ruined dwellings, now deprived of their purpose, searching for buried remnants of household goods, here salvaging a bit of tin or wire from the rubble, there picking up a few splinters of wood and stowing them in the bags they wore slung around them, which resembled botanical specimen containers."[63] There is a sparse assortment of junk for sale in the roofless shops: "Here a few jackets and trousers, belts with silver buckles, ties and brightly colored scarves were laid out, there a collection of shoes and boots of all kinds, often in very poor condition. Elsewhere hangers bore crumpled suits in various sizes, old-fashioned rustic smocks and jackets, along with darned stockings, socks and shirts, hats and hairnets, all on sale and jumbled up together."[64] However, the lowered standard of living and the reduced economic conditions that are evident as the empirical foundations of the narrative in such passages do not make up a comprehensive image of the world of the ruins. They are merely the setting for the paramount plan, which is to mythologize a reality that in its raw form defies description. Consequently the fleets of bombers also appear as transreal entities. "As if at the prompting of Indra, whose cruelty in destruction surpasses the demonic powers, they rose, the teeming messengers of death, to destroy the halls and houses of the great cities in murderous wars, a hundred times stronger than ever before, striking like the apocalypse."[65] Green-masked figures, members of a secret sect who give off a stale odor of gas and may be meant to symbolize the victims murdered in the camps, are introduced (with allegorical exaggeration) in dispute with the bogeymen of power who, inflated to over life size, proclaim a blasphemous dominion, until they collapse in on themselves, empty husks in uniform, leaving behind a diabolical stench. In the closing passages of the novel an attempt to make sense of the senseless is added to this mise-en-scène, which is almost worthy of Syberberg and owes its existence to the most dubious aspects of Expressionist fantasy. The longest-serving thinker in Kasack's kingdom of the dead indicates "that for some time the thirty-three initiates have been concentrating their forces on opening up and extending the region of Asia, so long cut off, for reincarnations, and they now seem to be intensifying their efforts by including the West too as an area for the resurrection of mind and body. This exchange of Asiatic and European ideas, hitherto only a gradual and sporadic process, is clearly perceptible in a series of phenomena."[66] It emerges, from further pronouncements by the Master Mage who is the highest instance of wisdom and authority in Kasack's novel, that millions must die in this wholesale operation, "to make room for those surging forward to be reborn. A vast number of people were called away prematurely, so that they could rise again when the time came as a growing crop, apocryphally reborn in a living space previously inaccessible to them." The choice of words and terminology in passages such as this, which are not rare in Kasack's epic, shows with alarming clarity that the secret language supposedly cultivated by the "internal emigrants" was to a high degree identical with the code of the Fascist intellectual world.[67] It is painful for a modern reader to see Kasack ignoring the appalling reality of collective catastrophe, very much in the style of his time, by invoking pseudo-humanist and Far Eastern philosophical notions, with a great deal of Symbolist jargon, and using the whole structure of his novel to place himself in the elevated company of those purely intellectual figures who preserve the memory of mankind in their function as archivists in the city beyond the river. In *Nekyia,* Nossack too succumbs to the temptation to make the real horrors of the time disappear through the artifice of abstraction and metaphysical fraudulence. *Nekyia,* like *Die Stadt hinter dem Strom,* is the account of a journey to the kingdom of the dead, and like Kasack's novel the book contains teachers, mentors, masters, ancestors both male and female, much patriarchalist discipline and much prenatal obscurity. We are in the midst of that pedagogic province which, in the German tradition, extends from Goethe's idealistic vision in *Wilhelm Meister* of a community devoted to self-improvement, through Stefan George's *Stern des Bundes* ("Star of the League"), and on to Stauffenberg and Himmler. If this idea of an elite operating outside and above the state as the guardian of secret knowledge reemerges, even though it had so utterly discredited itself in social practice, and if it does so in order to enlighten those who barely escaped total destruction with their lives about the presumed metaphysical meaning of their experience, we are looking at evidence of a profound ideological inflexibility going far beyond the minds of individual authors, an inflexibility for which only a steadfast gaze bent on reality can compensate.

It is undoubtedly to Nossack's credit that in spite of his unfortunate tendency to indulge in philosophical exaggeration and false notions of transcendence, he was the only writer of the time to try recording what he actually saw as plainly as possible. Even in his account of the destruction of Hamburg, it is true, the rhetoric of fatefulness sometimes intrudes—he speaks of a human countenance sanctified for the transit to eternity,[68] and matters finally take a turn towards fairy tale and allegory—but on the whole he is primarily concerned with plain facts: the season of the year, the weather, the observer's viewpoint, the drone of the approaching squadrons, the red firelight on the horizon, the physical and mental condition of refugees from the cities, the burnt-out scenery, chimneys that curiously still remain standing, washing put out to dry on a rack outside a kitchen window, a torn net curtain blowing from an empty veranda, a living room sofa with a crochet cover, countless other objects lost forever, the rubble burying them and the dreadful new life moving beneath it, people's sudden craving for perfume. On the whole, the moral imperative for at least *one* writer to describe what happened in Hamburg on that night in July leads him to abandon elaboration. His account, given in dispassionate language, tells of "a terrible event in prehistoric times."[69] A group of people were burnt to death in a bombproof shelter because the doors had jammed, and coal stored in the cellars next to it caught fire. So it had been. "They had all fled from the hot walls to the middle of the cellar. They were found there crowded together, bloated with the heat."[70] The narrative tone here is that of the messenger in classical tragedy. Nossack knows that such messengers are often strung up for their pains. Inserted into his account of the fall of Hamburg is the parable of a man who claims that he must speak of what actually happened, and whose audience kills him for the deathly chill he spreads. Those who can salvage some metaphysical meaning from the destruction are usually spared such a wretched fate; their trade is less dangerous than dealing in concrete memory. Elias Canetti, in an essay on the diary of Dr. Hachiya from Hiroshima, asks what it means to survive such a vast catastrophe, and says that the answer can be gauged only from a text which, like Hachiya's observations, is notable for precision and responsibility. "If there were any point," writes Canetti, "in wondering what form of literature is essential to a thinking, seeing human being today, then it is this."[71] The same may be said of Nossack's account of the destruction of the city of Hamburg, which is unique even in his own work.

The ideal of truth inherent in its entirely unpretentious objectivity, at least over long passages, proves itself the only legitimate reason for continuing to produce literature in the face of total destruction. Conversely, the construction of aesthetic or pseudo-aesthetic effects from the ruins of an annihilated world is a process depriving literature of its right to exist.

As an example, it would be difficult to surpass the page after page of embarrassing writing in Peter de Mendelssohn's *Die Kathedrale,* which lay unpublished for a long time (and a good thing too, one is tempted to say), and even after publication attracted little notice. It begins with the hero of the story, Torstenson, coming up from a cellar buried under debris on the morning after a heavy air raid. "He was sweating; the pulse was throbbing in his temples. Dear God, he thought, this is appalling; I'm not a young man anymore; ten years ago, five years ago this kind of thing wouldn't have bothered me in the least, but now I'm forty-one, healthy, fit, practically uninjured while the whole world seems to be dead around me, my hands are shaking and my knees are trembling, and it's as much as I can do to work myself out of this rubble. And indeed everyone around him did appear to be dead; there was total silence; he called out a couple of times—was there anybody there?—but no answer came from the darkness."[72] Mendelssohn goes on in this fashion, lurching between grammatical infelicities and a derivative style, not without citing all manner of horrors as if to show that he does not shrink from depicting the reality of destruction in its most drastic aspects. Even so, an unfortunate tendency towards melodrama remains dominant. Torstenson sees "the head of an old woman forced, all awry, into a broken window frame," and fears that in the dark his nailed boots might "slip on the ebbing warmth of a woman's crushed breast."[73] Torstenson fears, Torstenson sees, Torstenson thought, had the impression that, was in some doubt as to whether, judged that, was at odds with himself, was disinclined—it is from this egomaniacal viewpoint, necessarily maintained by the mechanism of the novel as it clatters along, that we are obliged to follow a plot which obviously borrowed its grandiose triviality from the screenplays written by Thea von Harbou for Fritz Lang, more particularly the script for the mega-production *Metropolis*. Thus the arrogance of technological man is also one of the main themes of Mendelssohn's novel. As a young architect—and despite the author's disclaimer, echoes of Heinrich Tessenow and his star pupil, Albert Speer, are no coincidence—Torstenson had built the great cathedral that is now the only building still standing among the rubble.

The second dimension of the narrative is its eroticism. Torstenson is in search of his first love, Karena, the gravedigger's beautiful daughter, now probably lying buried beneath the ruins. Like Maria in *Metropolis,* Karena is a saint perverted by the ruling powers. Torstenson remembers their first meeting at the bookseller Kafka's; Kafka, like the necromancer Rotwang in Lang's film, lives in a crooked house full of books and trapdoors. That winter evening, Torstenson recollects, Karena was wearing a hood that seemed to burn from within. "The red lining and the golden strands of hair on her cheeks had merged into a wreath of flames framing her face, which remained still and untouched, and even seemed to be smiling slightly"[74]—no doubt another version of the saintly Maria of the catacombs, who later mutates into a robot woman and enters the service of Fredersen, the lord of Metropolis. Karena commits a similar act of betrayal in choosing to side with Gossensass, the new ruler, when Torstenson goes into exile. According to Mendelssohn, the book was to end with Torstenson putting out to sea in one of the great barges used to clear the ruins; as the rubble sinks into the depths, he sees the whole city down on the seabed, complete and undamaged, another Atlantis. "All that was destroyed above is intact down here, and everything that is left standing up above, in particular the cathedral, is absent down here."[75] Torstenson climbs down a flight of steps in the water and into the sunken city, where he is arrested and must plead for his life before a court of law—another fantastic vision very much in the style of Thea von Harbou. The choreography of the masses, the march of victorious armies into the destroyed city, the move of the surviving population into the cathedral, all bear the Lang/Harbou trademark, and so does the repeated intensification of plot elements, creating an effect of kitsch that offends against all literary criteria. Torstenson, who encounters an orphan boy at the beginning of the novel, soon comes upon a seventeen-year-old girl just out of a penal camp. When they meet for the first time on the steps of the cathedral "in the bright sunlight" the rags of her dress slip off her shoulders, and Torstenson studies her, we are told, "calmly and thoroughly." "She was a dirty, grubby girl, beaten black and blue, with tangled black hair, but in her slender and supple youth she was lovely as a goddess from the groves of antiquity."[76] Appropriately, it then turns out that the girl's name is Aphrodite Homeriades, and (to provide an additional frisson) she is a Greek Jew from Salonika. Torstenson, who at first contemplates sleeping with this strange beauty himself, finally and in a kind of reconciliation scene leads her to the orphaned German boy so that she can teach him the secret of life—another echo, one might well think, of the final frames of *Metropolis,* which are shot outside the gateway of a mighty cathedral. It is not easy to sum up the quantities of lasciviousness and ultra-German racial kitsch Mendelssohn offers his readers (with, we must assume, the best of intentions), but in any case his wholesale fictionalization of the theme of the ruined city is the opposite of the prosaic sobriety for which Nossack strives in the best passages of his record, *Der Untergang* ("The End"). Where Nossack successfully exercises deliberate restraint in his approach to the horrors unleashed by Operation Gomorrah, Mendelssohn plunges headlong into more than two hundred pages of trash.

A literary approach to the reality of the destruction of a very different kind, but similarly dubious, comes towards the end of Arno Schmidt's short novel *Aus dem Leben eines Fauns* ("Scenes from the Life of a Faun"), published in 1953. It may appear rather discourteous to point out the failings of a writer who later became a meritorious Academy president, and one might well be particularly reluctant to cast aspersions on the reputation of Schmidt, that most uncompromising artist in words. Nonetheless, I think it is fair to query the dynamic linguistic action with which he stages the spectacle of an air raid in this book. The author certainly intended to conjure up a striking image of the eddying whirlpool of destruction with his exaggerated language, but I for one, reading a passage like the following, do not visualize the supposed subject: life at the terrible moment of its disintegration. "*A buried tank of alcohol shook itself loose,* rolled out like a sheet of mica on a hot hand, and dissolved in a donnybrook (out of which fiery brooks flowed: a dismayed policeman commanded the one on his right to halt and was vaporized in the line of duty). A fat-lady cloud stood up above the warehouse, puffed out her round belly and belched a pastry head high into the air, laughed throatily: so what!, and rumbling the while knotted up her arms and legs, turned toward us in steatopygically, and farted whole sheaves of hot iron tubing, endlessly, the virtuosa, till the shrubs beside us curtsied low and babbled."[77] I do not see what is being described; all I see is the author, eager and persistent, intent on his linguistic fretwork. Once people practicing some craft as a hobby have developed a technique, they typically keep producing the same thing over and over again, and even in this extreme case Schmidt is the cobbler doggedly sticking to his last. We get the kaleidoscopic dissolution of contours, an anthropomorphic vision of nature, mica plucked from the card index, various lexical rarities, grotesquerie, metaphor, humor, onomatopoeia, the vulgar and the high-flown, violence and explosiveness and noise. I do not think my dislike for the ostentatious avantgardist style of Schmidt's study of the moment of destruction derives from a fundamentally conservative attitude to form and language, for unlike this five-finger exercise the discontinuous notes made by Jäcki in Hubert Fichte's novel *Detlevs Imitationen "Grünspan"* ("Detlev's Imitations") during his researches on the Hamburg raid seem to me a very plausible literary approach, probably mainly because they are not abstract and imaginary in character, but concrete and documentary. It is with this documentary approach, which has an early precursor in

Nossack's *Der Untergang,* that German postwar literature really comes into its own and begins the serious study of material incommensurable with traditional aesthetics. Fichte's book is set in 1968, the twenty-fifth anniversary of the raid on Hamburg. Jäcki finds a small volume of "thick, quince-yellow pre–currency reform paper" in the library of the Eppendorf Medical School. The title runs: "Findings of Pathological and Anatomical Investigations After the Raids on Hamburg in 1943–1945. With Thirty Illustrations and Eleven Plates." In the park—"Cool wind around lilac trees. In the background the cottage, tea room, piss house around which Alster queers swarm at night"—Jäcki leafs through the borrowed book: "b. The autopsy of the shriveled corpse. Available for examination consequently were heat-shriveled corpses with the attendant effects of more or less advanced decomposition. There was no question of a section with knife and scissors in the case of these shriveled corpses. First of all, the clothes had to be removed, which, given the exceptional stiffness of the bodies, was as a rule only to be accomplished by cutting or tearing and caused damage to individual parts of the body. Depending on the dryness of the joints, heads and extremities could frequently be broken off without difficulty, if they had remained attached to the body at all in the course of recovery and transport. Insofar as body cavities were not already exposed through destruction of the tegumen, the bone scissors or saw was required, in order to cut the hardened skin. Solidification and shrinkage of the inner organs prevented cutting with the knife; frequently the individual organs, especially the chest organs, could be broken out as a whole with windpipe, aorta, and carotid artery, with diaphragm, liver, or kidneys adhering. Organs which were in an advanced state of autolysis or had been completely hardened by the effects of heat were usually difficult to cut with the knife; decomposing, cheesy, claylike, buttery, or charred-crumbly masses of tissue or organ residues were broken, torn, crumbled, or plucked apart."[78] This medical account of the further destruction of a body already mummified by the firestorm shows a reality of which Schmidt's linguistic radicalism knows nothing. His elaborate style veils over the facts that stare straight at us in the language of those professionally involved in the horror, going about their work stolidly and without many scruples, perhaps, as Jäcki suspects, because the general mayhem provides them with an opportunity to add a feather or so to their caps. This document, a genuine one written in the interests of science by a certain Dr. Siegfried Gräff, opens up a view into the abyss of a mind armed against all contingencies. The informative value of such authentic documents, before which all fiction pales, also determines the character of Alexander Kluge's archaeological excavations of the slag-heaps of our collective existence. His account of the air raid on Halberstadt begins on April 8, when the

program of the Capitol cinema (which has been showing films for years and is about to screen *Heimkehr*—
"Homecoming"—with Paula Wessely and Attila Hörbiger) is interrupted by the prior claims of a program of
destruction, and the cinema's experienced employee
Frau Schrader is trying to clear up the rubble in time for
the two o'clock matinee. The quasi-humorous tone of this
passage, which I have already mentioned, arises from the
extreme discrepancy between the active and passive fields
of action involved in the catastrophe, and from the inadequacy of the automatic reactions of Frau Schrader, for
whom "the devastation of the right-hand side of the audi-
torium . . . [had] no meaningful or dramaturgical connection with the film being screened."[79] There is similar
irrationality in the description of a troop of soldiers sent
to dig up and sort out "100 corpses, some of them badly
mutilated,"[80] with no idea of the purpose of "this operation" in the present circumstances. The unknown photog-
rapher intercepted by a military patrol who claims that
"he wanted to record the burning city, his own home
town, in its hour of misfortune"[81] resembles Frau Schrader
in following his professional instincts. The only reason
why his declared intention of recording the very end is
not absurd is that the pictures he took, which Kluge
added to his text, have survived, as he could hardly have
expected at the time. The women on watch in the tower,
Frau Arnold and Frau Zacke, equipped with folding

HEIMKEHR

PAULA WESSELY · PETER PETERSEN · ATTILA HÖRBIGER

Ruth Hellberg, Berta Drews, Elsa Wagner, Gerhild Weber
Carl Raddatz, Werner Fütterer, Otto Wernicke

Drehbuch: Gerhard Menzel · Musik: Willy Schmidt-Gentner

Herstellungsgruppe: Erich von Neusser
SPIELLEITUNG: GUSTAV UCICKY

Ein Gustav Ucicky-Film der Wien-Film im Verleih der Ufa

chairs, torches, thermos flasks, packets of sandwiches, binoculars and radio sets, are still dutifully reporting as the tower itself seems to move beneath them and its wooden cladding begins to burn. Frau Arnold dies under a mountain of rubble with a bell on top of it, while Frau Zacke lies for hours with a broken thigh until she is rescued by people fleeing from the buildings on the Martiniplan. Twelve minutes after the air raid warning, a wedding party in the Zum Ross inn is buried, together with all its social differences and animosities—the bridegroom was from a prosperous family in Cologne, his bride, from Halberstadt, lower on the social scale. These and many of the other stories making up the text show how, even in the middle of the catastrophe, individuals and groups were still unable to assess the real degree of danger and abandon their usual roles. Since, as Kluge points out, normal time and "the sensory experience of time" were at odds with each other in the accelerating pace of the disaster, the people of Halberstadt, he says, could not have "devised practicable emergency measures . . . except with tomorrow's brains."[82] He does not mean that, conversely, it is useless to study the history of such catastrophes after the event. Instead, the retrospective learning process—and this is the raison d'être of Kluge's account, compiled thirty years later—is the only way of deflecting human wishful thinking towards the anticipation of a future that would not already be preempted by the anxieties arising from the suppression of experience. The primary-school teacher Gerda Baethe, a figure in Kluge's text, has similar ideas. It is true, the author comments, that to implement a "strategy from below" such as Gerda has in mind would have required "seventy thousand determined schoolteachers, all like her, each of them teaching hard for twenty years from 1918 onwards, in every country that had fought in the war."[83] Despite the ironic style, the prospect suggested here of an alternative historical outcome, possible in specific circumstances, is a serious call to work for the future in defiance of all calculations of probability. Central to Kluge's detailed description of the social organization of disaster, which is preprogrammed by the ever-recurrent and ever-intensifying errors of history, is the idea that a proper understanding of the catastrophes we are always setting off is the first prerequisite for the social organization of happiness. However, it is difficult to dismiss the idea that the systematic destruction Kluge sees arising from the development of the means and modes of industrial production hardly seems to justify the principle of hope. The construction of the strategy of air war in all its monstrous complexity, the transformation of bomber crews into professionals, "trained administrators of war in the air,"[84] the question of how to overcome the psychological problem of keeping them interested in their tasks despite the abstract nature of their function, the problems of conducting an orderly cycle of operations that involve "200 medium-sized industrial plants"[85] flying towards a city, and of the technology ensuring that the bombs would cause large-scale fires and firestorms—all these factors, which Kluge studies from the organizers' viewpoint, show that so much intelligence, capital, and labor went into the planning of destruction that, under the pressure of all the accumulated potential, it *had* to happen in the end. There is further evidence of the inevitability of such a development in a 1952 interview between the Halberstadt journalist Kunzert and Brigadier Frederick L. Anderson of the U.S. Eighth Army Air Force, which Kluge included in his text. In that interview Anderson looks, from the military viewpoint, at the question of whether hoisting a white flag made from six sheets on the tower of St. Martin's in good time might have prevented the bombing of the city. His comments culminate in a statement illustrating the notorious irrationality to which rational argument leads. He points out that the bombs they had brought were, after all, "expensive items." "In practice, they couldn't have been dropped over mountains or open country after so much labor had gone into making them at home."[86] The result of the prior claims of productivity, from which with the best will in the world neither responsible individuals nor groups could dissoci-

ate themselves, was the ruined city laid out before us in one of the photographs that Kluge included in his text. He adds a caption underneath, a quotation from Marx: "We see how the history of *industry* and the now *objective* existence of industry have become the *open* book of the *human consciousness,* human *psychology* perceived in sensory terms . . ." (Kluge's italics).[87] This is the history of industry as the open book of human thought and feeling—can materialistic epistemology or any other such theory be maintained in the face of such destruction? Is the destruction not, rather, irrefutable proof that the catastrophes which develop, so to speak, in our hands and seem to break out suddenly are a kind of experiment, anticipating the point at which we shall drop out of what we have thought for so long to be our autonomous history and back into the history of nature? "(The sun bears heavily down on the city, since there is hardly any shade.) After a few days, paths bearing some slight relation to the old road network are trodden over the sites piled high with rubble, the streets obliterated by the ruins. The silence above the ruins is striking. It seems as if nothing is going on, but appearances are deceptive insofar as fires are still burning in the cellars, moving underground from one coal hole to another. Many crawling creatures. Some parts of the city stink. There are groups out looking for corpses. A pungent, 'silent' smell of burning lies over the city; after a few days it feels 'familiar.' "[88] Here Kluge is looking down, both literally and metaphorically, from a vantage point above the destruction. The ironic amazement with which he registers the facts allows him to maintain the essential distance of an observer. Yet even Kluge, that most enlightened of writers, suspects that we are unable to learn from the misfortunes we bring on ourselves, that we are incorrigible and will continue along the beaten tracks that bear some slight relation to the old road network. For all Kluge's intellectual steadfastness, therefore, he looks at the destruction of his hometown with the horrified fixity of Walter Benjamin's "angel of history," whose "face is turned toward the past. Where we perceive a chain of events, he sees one single catastrophe which keeps piling wreckage upon wreckage and hurls it in front of his feet. The angel would like to stay, awaken the dead, make whole what has been smashed. But a storm is blowing from Paradise; it has got caught in his wings with such violence that the angel can no longer close them. This storm irresistibly propels him into the future to which his back is turned, while the pile of debris before him grows skyward. This storm is what we call progress."[89]

III

THE REACTION TO MY ZÜRICH LECTURES CALLS
for a postscript. I myself had intended what I said in
Zürich as merely a rough-and-ready collection of various
observations, materials, and theses, and I suspected that
in many respects it needed to be complemented and cor-
rected. In particular, I thought my claim that the destruction of German cities in the last years of the Second
World War had not registered in the consciousness of
the reemergent nation would be refuted by instances
which had escaped my notice. Not so; instead, everything
I was told in dozens of letters confirmed me in my belief
that if those born after the war were to rely solely on the
testimony of writers, they would scarcely be able to form
any idea of the extent, nature, and consequences of the

catastrophe inflicted on Germany by the air raids. Yes, there are a few relevant texts, but what little has been recorded in literature, in terms of both quantity and quality, stands in no relation to the extreme collective experiences of the time. The destruction of all the larger German cities and many of the smaller ones, which one must assume could hardly be overlooked at the time and which marks the face of the country to this day, is reflected in works written after 1945 by a self-imposed silence, an absence also typical of other areas of discourse, from family conversations to historical writings. It seems to me remarkable that the guild of German historians, known to be among the most industrious in the world, has not yet, so far as I am aware, produced a comprehensive or even an exploratory study of the subject. Only the military historian Jörg Friedrich, in Chapter 8 of his *Das Gesetz des Krieges* ("The Law of War"),[90] looks more closely at the evolution and consequences of the Allied strategy of destruction. Characteristically, however, his remarks have not aroused anything like the interest they deserve. This scandalous deficiency, which has become ever clearer to me over the years, reminded me that I had grown up with the feeling that something was being kept from me: at home, at school, and by the German writers whose books I read hoping to glean more information about the monstrous events in the background of my own life.

I spent my childhood and youth on the northern outskirts of the Alps, in a region that was largely spared the immediate effects of the so-called hostilities. At the end of the war I was just one year old, so I can hardly have any impressions of that period of destruction based on personal experience. Yet to this day, when I see photographs or documentary films dating from the war I feel as if I were its child, so to speak, as if those horrors I did not experience cast a shadow over me, and one from which I shall never entirely emerge. A book on the history of the little market town of Sonthofen, published in 1963 to celebrate its gaining civic status, contains a passage which runs: "The war took much from us, but our beautiful native landscape was left untouched, as flourishing as ever."[91] Reading that sentence, I see pictures merging before my mind's eye—paths through the fields, river meadows, and mountain pastures mingling with images of destruction—and oddly enough, it is the latter, not the now entirely unreal idylls of my early childhood, that make me feel rather as if I were coming home, perhaps because they represent the more powerful and dominant reality of my first years of life. I know now that at the time, when I was lying in my bassinet on the balcony of the Seefeld house and looking up at the pale blue sky, there was a pall of smoke in the air all over Europe, over the rearguard actions in east and west, over the ruins of the German cities, over the camps where untold numbers of people were burnt, people from Berlin and Frank-

Viel hat uns der Krieg genommen, doch uns blieb – unberührt und blühend wie eh und je – unsere herrliche Heimatlandschaft.

Und allmählich schritten wir wieder – begleitet vom Lachen unserer Kinder – in eine hoffnungsfrohe Zukunft.

furt, from Wuppertal and Vienna, from Würzburg and Kissingen, from Hilversum and The Hague, Naumur and Thionville, Lyon and Bordeaux, Kraków and Łódź, Szeged and Sarajevo, Salonika and Rhodes, Ferrara and Venice—there was scarcely a place in Europe from which

no one had been deported to his death in those years. I have seen memorial tablets even in the most remote villages on the island of Corsica reading "Morte à Auschwitz" or "Tué par les Allemands, Flossenburg 1944." I saw something else in Corsica too—if I may be permitted a digression: I saw the picture from my parents' bedroom in the church of Morosaglia, a half-decayed edifice with a dusty, pseudo-Baroque interior. It was a bluish oleograph in the Nazarene style, showing Christ before his Passion seated deep in thought in the moonlit, nocturnal Garden of Gethsemane. The selfsame picture had hung over my parents' conjugal bed for many years, and then at some point it disappeared, probably when they bought new bedroom furniture. And now here it was again, or at least one exactly like it, in the village church of Morosaglia, General Paoli's birthplace, leaning against the plinth of an altar in a dark corner of one of the side aisles. My parents told me that just before their wedding in 1936 they had bought their picture in Bamberg, where my father was transport sergeant in the cavalry regiment in which the young Stauffenberg had begun his military career ten years earlier. Such is the dark backward and abysm of time. Everything lies all jumbled up in it, and when you look down you feel dizzy and afraid.

In one of my narratives I have described how in 1952, when I moved with my parents and siblings from my birthplace of Wertach to Sonthofen, nineteen kilometers away, nothing seemed as fascinating as the presence of areas of waste land here and there among the rows of houses, for ever since I had been to Munich, as I said in that passage, few things were so clearly linked in my mind with the word "city" as mounds of rubble, cracked walls, and empty windows through which you saw the empty air. On February 22 and April 29, 1945, bombs had been dropped on the totally insignificant little market town of Sonthofen, probably because the place contained two large barracks for the mountain troops and the artillery, as well as an establishment known as the Ordensburg, one of three training colleges set up for the formation of the new Fascist elite directly after the Nazis came to power. As for the air raids on Sonthofen, I remember when I was fourteen or fifteen asking the parson who taught religious

education at the Oberstdorf Gymnasium how we could reconcile our ideas of divine providence with the fact that neither the barracks nor the Ordensburg had been destroyed during this air raid, only, and as if in place of them, the parish church and the church of the hospital foundation, but I do not remember what he said in reply. In any case, the fact remained that after the raids on Sonthofen the five hundred or so local men who had fallen or been posted missing in the war were joined by about a hundred civilian victims, including, as I once noted,

Elisabeth Zobel, Regina Salvermooser, Carlo Moltrasia, Konstantin Sohnczak, Seraphine Buchenberger, Cäzilie Fügenschuh, and Viktoria Stürmer, a nun in the Altenspital whose religious name was Mother Sebalda. Of the buildings destroyed in Sonthofen and not rebuilt until the early 1960s, I remember two in particular. One was the railway terminal station, the main part of which was used as a storehouse for rolls of cable, telegraph poles, and similar items, while Gogl the music teacher gave lessons to some of his pupils every evening in the largely undamaged extension building. It was strange, especially in winter, to see the music pupils scraping away with their bows at their violas and cellos in the one lighted room of that ruined building, as if they were sitting on a raft drifting away into the darkness. The other ruin still present in my mind was the building known as the Herz-Schloss close to the Protestant church, a villa built at the turn of the century. Nothing was left of it now but its cast-iron garden railings and the cellars. By the 1950s the plot of land, where a few handsome trees had survived the catastrophe, was entirely overgrown, and as children we often spent whole afternoons in this wilderness created in the middle of town by the war. I remember that I never felt at ease going down the steps to the cellars. They smelled of damp and decay, and I always feared I might bump into the body of an animal or a human corpse. A few years later, a self-service shop opened on the site of the Herz-Schloss, an ugly, windowless single-story building, and the once beautiful garden of the villa finally disappeared under the tarmac of a car park. That, reduced to its lowest common denominator, is the main theme of the history of postwar Germany. When I first came back from England to Sonthofen at the end of the 1960s I shuddered at the sight of the fresco showing foodstuffs on the exterior wall of the self-service shop (for advertising purposes, apparently). It measured about six by two meters, and depicted an enormous platter of sliced cold meats, as served on every self-respecting supper table at the time, in colors from blood red to rose pink.

But I do not necessarily have to return to Germany and my place of origin to visualize that period of destruction. It often comes back to my mind where I live at present. Many of the more than seventy airfields from which the war of annihilation was waged against Germany were in the county of Norfolk. Some ten of them are still military bases, and a few others are now used by flying clubs, but most were abandoned after the war. Grass has grown over the runways, and the dilapidated control towers, bunkers, and corrugated iron huts stand in an often eerie landscape where you sense the dead souls of the men who never came back from their missions, and of those who perished in the vast fires. I live very close to Seething airfield. I sometimes walk my dog there, and imagine what the place was like when the aircraft took off with their heavy

DORNIER CREW LEFT TO RIGHT, (9 MAY 42)
UFFZ BM ALBERT OTTERBACH   AGED   21
SSFW BU RUDOLF BUCKSCH   29
OBLT FF WERNER BOLLERT   30
                              BIRTHDAY 18 MAY 1911
UFFZ BF MATHIAS SPEUSER   22

freight and flew out over the sea, making for Germany. Two
years before these flights began, a Luftwaffe Dornier plane
crashed in a field not far from my house during a raid on
Norwich. One of the four crew members who lost their
lives, Lieutenant Bollert, shared a birthday with me and
was the same age as my father.

So much for the few points at which my own life
touches the history of the air war. Entirely insignificant in
themselves, they have nonetheless haunted my mind, and
finally impelled me to go at least a little way into the question of why German writers would not or could not describe the destruction of the German cities as millions
experienced it. I am well aware that my unsystematic
notes do not do justice to the complexity of the subject,

but I think that even in their incomplete form they cast some light on the way in which memory (individual, collective and cultural) deals with experiences exceeding what is tolerable. To judge by the letters I have received, it also seems to me as if my tentative observations hit a sensitive spot in the intellectual makeup of the German nation. As soon as the Swiss newspapers reported my Zürich lectures I had a great many inquiries from the German press and from radio and television companies, asking whether they could print extracts from what I had said, or whether I was prepared to discuss the subject further in interviews. I also heard from private individuals wanting to read my Zürich texts. Some of these requests were motivated by a need to see the Germans depicted, for once, as victims. Other letters claimed that my thesis was based on inadequate information, and pointed out such sources as Erich Kästner's 1946 reports from Berlin, or local history collections, or academic research work. A professor emerita from Greifswald who had read the *Neue Zürcher Zeitung* report complained that Germany was still divided into two. My claims, she wrote, were yet more evidence that the West neither knows nor wants to know anything about the other German culture, for the subject of the air war, she said, was not ignored in the former DDR and there were annual commemorations of the raid on Dresden. The lady in Greifswald seemed to have no idea of the way the fall of that city was exploited in the official rhetoric of the East German state, as Günter Jäckel describes it in his essay in the *Dresdner Hefte* on the events of February 13, 1945.[92]

Dr. Hans Joachim Schröder wrote to me from Hamburg with part of his thousand-page study, published by Niemeyer in 1992 as *Die gestohlenen Jahre—Erzählgeschichten und Geschichtserzählung im Interview: Der zweite Weltkrieg aus der Sicht ehemaliger Mannschaftssoldaten* ("The Stolen Years—Narratives and History in Interviews: The Second World War as Seen by Former Soldiers"). He sent me the seventh chapter, which covers the fall of Hamburg, and according to Dr. Schröder shows that collective memory of the air raids is not quite as dead in Germany as I supposed. Far be it from me to doubt that witnesses of the time remember a great deal, and that it can be brought to light in interviews. On the other hand, the records of such interviews run along surprisingly stereotyped lines. Among the central problems of "eyewitness reports" are their inherent inadequacy, notorious unreliability, and curious vacuity: their tendency to follow a set routine and go over and over the same material. Dr. Schröder's studies largely ignore the psychological aspect of the recall of traumatic experiences, with the result that he can treat even the extraordinarily sinister account given by the real-life anatomist of the shriveled corpses, Dr. Siegfried Gräff, which features prominently in Hubert Fichte's novel *Detlevs Imitationen "Grünspan,"* as merely one of many documents, and he remains apparently immune to the cynicism, so perfectly conveyed in that text, of those who were professionally involved with horror. I repeat, I do not doubt that there were and are memories of those nights of destruction; I simply do not trust the form—including the literary form—in which they are expressed, and I do not believe they were a significant factor in the public consciousness of the new Federal Republic in any sense except as encouraging the will to reconstruction.

In a reader's letter on Volker Hage's article in *Der Spiegel* on my Zürich lectures, Dr. Joachim Schultz of Bayreuth University points out that in looking, with his students, at books for young people written between 1945 and 1960, he came upon more or less extensive memories of the nights of bombing, and that therefore my diagnosis applied at most only to highbrow adult literature. I have not read the books he mentions, but I can hardly imagine that a genre specifically for young people had hit upon the right dimensions for description of the German catastrophe. Most of the letters I received were promoting some specific interest, although seldom as frankly as in the case of a senior teacher in a West German city who wrote me a long screed after coming across a piece I had published on the subject in the *Frankfurter Rundschau*. As it turned out Herr K., who shall remain nameless, was not particularly interested in the air war;

instead, he seized the opportunity—first paying me a few compliments with scarcely concealed rancor—to accuse me of bad syntactical habits. Herr K. was particularly annoyed by the placing of the predicate at the front of a phrase, which he regards as the chief symptom of the increasingly common use of simplified German. He writes to say that he finds me falling into this bad habit, which he calls asthmatic syntax, on every third page, and he demands an account of the point and purpose of my constant offenses against correct linguistic usage. He also cites several of his other linguistic hobbyhorses, explicitly describing himself as an "enemy to all anglicisms" in German, although he does concede that "fortunately" there were few of those in my work. Herr K. enclosed with his letter several peculiar poems and notes, with titles such as "More from Herr K." and "Yet more from Herr K.," which I read with no small degree of concern.

In the rest of the mail I received I also found samples of all kinds of literary items, sometimes in manuscript, sometimes privately printed for family and friends. They almost seemed to confirm the opinion expressed by Gerhard Keppner (of Seebruck) in a letter to *Der Spiegel*. "We must remember," writes Herr Keppner, "that a nation of 86 million, once praised as a people of philosophers and poets, experienced the worst catastrophe of its recent history with the destruction of its cities, when mil-

lions were driven from their homes. It is difficult to believe that no mighty echo of these events reverberated in
literature. And in fact it did, but little of that literature
was published—it was put away in drawers. Who but the
media erected this wall of taboo . . . and are still main-
taining it?" Whatever Herr Keppner may think—and
there is a faint touch of paranoia about his remarks, as
with many of the letters from readers—the writings I was
sent cannot be said to represent a mighty if subterranean
echo of the collapse of the Reich and the destruction of its
cities. They tend instead to be rather cheerful reminiscences, marked by those characteristic turns of phrase
that unintentionally express a certain social alignment
and state of mind, and fill me with the utmost uneasiness
wherever I come upon them. We have here the glorious
world of our mountains, the carefree eye resting upon the
beauty of our homeland, the holy days of Christmas (so
successfully appropriated and colonized by the Nazis), Alf
the German shepherd dog, quite beside himself when
Dorle Breitschneider calls for his mistress ("Frauchen" is
the frightful term used) and they all go for a walk; with
scarcely concealed nostalgia the writers dwell on their
past lives and emotions: the sense of togetherness enjoyed
over *Kaffee und Kuchen*. We are told how Granny still works
all hours in house and garden, and hear of various gentle-
men who came for dinner and—most hair-raising of all

German clichés—*zum gemütlichen Beisammensein;** Karl is in Africa now, Fritz is in the east, baby Bübchen is running around the garden naked as the day he was born; our thoughts are with our boys in Stalingrad now; Granny writes from Fallingbostel, Father has fallen in Russia; we only hope the German border will keep at bay the tide sweeping in from the steppes; getting hold of food has become the main preoccupation these days; Mother and Hiltrud have found lodgings with a master baker, and so on, and so forth. It is difficult to define the kind of distortion that continues to make itself felt in retrospective accounts of this kind, but it must be something to do with the particular form taken by petit bourgeois life in Germany. The case histories presented by Alexander and Margarete Mitscherlich in their *Die Unfähigkeit zu trauern* ("The Inability to Mourn") make one at least suspect some connection between the German catastrophe ushered in under Hitler's regime and the regulation of intimate feelings within the German family. At any rate, the more of these reminiscences I read, the more likely it seems that there were psychosocial origins to the aberration which developed with such momentous consequences. The writings also contain genuine insights, attempts at self-criticism, and moments when the dreadful truth makes its way to the surface, but usually they quickly revert to the harm-

---

*Approximately, "for a cozy get-together."

less, conversational tone that is so strikingly dispropor-
tionate to the reality of the time.

A number of the letters and accounts that reached me
did deviate from the basic pattern of family reminiscence,
showing traces of uneasiness and distress still emerging
today in the minds of their writers. A lady from Wies-
baden, who says that as a child she always kept particularly quiet during air raids, writes of the panic terror with
which she later reacted to the ringing of an alarm clock,
the screech of circular saws, the sound of thunderstorms,
and the banging of party poppers. Another letter, written
in haste—indeed, breathlessly—while its sender was on a
journey somewhere, pours out fragmented memories of
nights spent in the bunkers and underground railway tun-
nels of Berlin, images frozen in time, the disconnected
comments of people talking about the jewelry they must
save, or the salted beans lying in a tub at home; a woman
with her hands closed convulsively on the Bible in her lap,
an old man clutching a bedside lamp that for some un-
fathomable reason he had brought down with him. The
letter, barely legible in places, emphasizes this clinging
and clutching with double exclamation marks, speaking of
"my trembling, my fears, my rage—still here in my head."

From Zürich I received a dozen pages from Harald
Hollenstein, son of a German mother and a Swiss father,
who spent his childhood in Hamburg and has tales to tell
of everyday life under National Socialism. "Let all good

Germans coming here / Announce 'Heil Hitler' loud and clear," read the lines in runic script up on an enamel plaque in every shop. He also writes about the first raids on Hamburg. At first, he says, not much happened. "Not in our neighborhood. Harburg harbor was the target only once: they were aiming for the oil tanks there. When we came up from the air raid shelter that night—I was still drowsy, abruptly woken from sleep for the second time— and we were out in the street again, we saw flames leaping into the black sky on the horizon over by the harbor. I watched the play of colors, fascinated, the red and yellow of the flames mingling against the background of the dark night sky and then separating again. Even later, I never saw such a clean, brilliant yellow, such a bright red, such a radiant orange. . . . Today, 55 years later, I think that sight was my most impressive experience of the whole war. I stood in the street for minutes on end watching this symphony of slowly changing colors. I never again saw such deep, bright colors, not in any painter's work. And if I had been a painter myself . . . it would have taken me a lifetime to search for those pure colors." Involuntarily, reading these lines, one wonders why no one, in contrast to those who wrote of the Great Fire of London or the fire of Moscow, described the burning German cities. "Rumor has it," writes Chateaubriand in his *Mémoires d'outre-tombe* ("Memories from Beyond the Grave"), "that the Kremlin has been undermined. . . . The various fires are spreading, feeding on each other, joining together. The tower of the arsenal burns like a tall candle in the middle of a blazing shrine. The Kremlin is only a black island on which the waves of the sea of flames break. In the glare reflected by the fires, the sky looks as if the Northern Lights were pulsing through it." In the city around him, Chateaubriand continues, "you hear stone vaults crack and burst; belfries with rivers of molten ore flowing down from them bend, totter, and collapse. Planks, rafters, and falling roofs sink cracking and spluttering into a Phlegethon, where they send up a glowing wave and millions of golden sparks." Chateaubriand's description is not an eyewitness account but a purely aesthetic reconstruction. It was out of the question to imagine such catastrophic panoramas of the German cities in flames in retrospect, probably because of the horror that so many experienced and perhaps never really overcame. The boy who grew up in Hamburg goes to Switzerland when the major raids begin, but later his mother tells him what she saw. She had to go to the Moorweide with a mass transport. "There was a bunker built in the middle of the meadow, said to be bombproof, made of concrete with a pitched roof. . . . Fourteen hundred people took shelter there after the first night of terror. The bunker received a direct hit and burst apart. The extent of what happened then must have been apocalyptic. . . . Hundreds of people outside, including my mother, were waiting to be taken to an assembly camp in Pinneberg. To reach the trucks, they had to climb over mountains of corpses, some completely dismembered, all lying around on the meadow among the remains of the former bombproof bunker. Many could not help vomiting when they saw the scene, many vomited as they trampled over the dead, others collapsed and lost consciousness. So my mother told me."

This secondhand memory going back over half a century is horrible enough, yet it is only a tiny part of what we do not know. Many who fled to the most remote parts of the Reich after the raids on Hamburg were in a demented state of mind. In one of my lectures I had quoted a passage from the diary of Friedrich Reck, who describes the corpse of a child falling out of a suitcase belonging to one of these deranged women from Hamburg when it springs open. Although, as I said in my rather baffled comments, it is difficult to think of a reason why Reck should have invented this grotesque scene, it is also hard to fit it into any framework of reality, so that one feels some doubt of its authenticity. But some time ago I was in Sheffield, where I met an elderly gentleman who, because of his Jewish origins, had been forced to leave his native Sonthofen and emigrate to England. His wife, who came to England immediately after the war, grew up in Stralsund. A midwife by profession, this resolute lady is extremely down-to-earth and not given to flights of fancy. After the Hamburg firestorm, in the summer of 1943 when she was sixteen years old, she was on duty as a volunteer helper at Stralsund railway station when a special train came in carrying refugees, most of them still utterly beside themselves, unable to speak of what had happened, struck dumb or sobbing and weeping with despair. And several of the women on this train from Hamburg, I heard quite recently on my visit to Sheffield, actually did have dead children in their luggage, children who had suffocated in the smoke or died in some other way during the air raid. We do not know what became of the mothers who fled carrying such burdens, whether and how they managed to readjust to normal life. Yet perhaps such fragmentary memories show that it is impossible to gauge the depths of trauma suffered by those who came away from the epicenters of the catastrophe. The right to silence claimed by the majority of these people is as inviolable as that of the survivors of Hiroshima, of whom Kenzaburo Oe says, in his notes on the city written in 1965, that even twenty years after the bomb fell many of them still could not speak of what happened that day.[93]

One man who tried to do so wrote to me saying that for years he had nurtured the project of writing a novel about Berlin to help him work through his earliest childhood memories. One of these childhood impressions—probably the key experience—was an air raid on the city. "I was lying in a laundry basket, the sky cast a red light a long way down the corridor, in this red twilight my mother put her terrified face close to mine, and when I was carried down to the cellar the rafters above me rose and swayed."[94] The author of these lines is Hans Dieter Schäfer, now a lecturer in German studies at Regensburg. Seeking to exhume the horrors of his childhood, Schäfer went to libraries and archives, filled many folders with material, drew up a topography of the locations from a 1933 Grieben Travel Guide, and flew to Berlin on frequent visits. "The aircraft," he notes in his account of the failure of his project, "hovered above the city; it was an August evening, and consequently the Müggelsee glowed with crimson light while the Spree was already in darkness. I remember that the angel on the victory column seemed to move its heavy cast-iron wings and look up at me with malicious curiosity; dusk was gathering beneath the television tower on Alexanderplatz, the shop display windows gave off an eerie glare, and the gloom sank slowly over the West and away to Charlottenburg, while the water of the lakes shone mildly in our eyes; the closer we came to land, the more frantically did endless streams of traffic race around; I turned to my other side and saw ducks flying in a kind of plow formation over the Zoo. A little later I was standing at its entrance, as if lost. Elephants tugged at their iron chains beneath somber trees, and over in the darkness ears were pricked and heard me coming."[95]

The Zoo was to have been one of the main subjects of

Schäfer's description of his many moments, hours, and years of terror in childhood. Yet he says that as he wrote he never succeeded "in recalling the full force of those dreadful events." "The more determination I brought to my quest, the more clearly I realized how hard it is for memory to make any headway."[96] As for the Zoo itself, a volume of material edited by Schäfer, *Berlin im zweiten Weltkrieg*[97] ("Berlin in the Second World War") gives some idea of what he might have had in mind. The chapter "Area Bombing, November 22–26, 1943" contains extracts from two books (Katharina Heinroth, *Mit Faltern begann's—Mein Leben mit Tieren in Breslau, München und Berlin* ["It Began with Butterflies—My Life with Animals in Breslau, Munich, and Berlin"; Munich, 1979], and Lutz Heck, *Tiere—Mein Abenteuer. Erlebnisse in Wildnis und Zoo* ["Animals—My Adventure: Experiences in the Wild and at the Zoo"; Vienna, 1952]), which paint a picture of the devastation of the Zoo by the air raids. Incendiary bombs and canisters of phosphorus set fire to fifteen of the Zoo buildings. The antelope house and the enclosure for the beasts of prey, the administration building and the director's villa were entirely destroyed, while the monkey house, the quarantine building, the main restaurant and the elephants' Indian temple were left in ruins or badly damaged. A third of the animals died—there were still two thousand left, although many had been evacuated. Deer and monkeys escaped; birds flew away through the broken glass roofs. "There were rumors," writes Heinroth, "that lions on the loose were prowling around the nearby Kaiser Wilhelm Memorial Church, but in fact they lay charred and suffocated in their cages."[98] Next day the ornamental three-story aquarium building and the thirty-meter crocodile hall were also destroyed, along with the artificial jungle. The great reptiles, writhing in pain, writes Heck, now lay beneath chunks of concrete, earth, broken glass, fallen palms and tree trunks, in water a foot deep, or crawled down the visitors' staircase, while the firelight of the dying city of Berlin shone red through a gate knocked off its hinges in the background. The elephants who had perished in the ruins of their sleeping quarters had to be cut up where they lay over the next few days, and Heck describes men crawling around inside the rib cages of the huge pachyderms and burrowing through mountains of entrails. These images of horror fill us with particular revulsion because they go beyond those routine accounts of human suffering that are to some extent precensored. And it may be that the horror which comes over us in reading such passages is also aroused by the recollection that zoos, which all over Europe owe their existence to a desire to demonstrate princely or imperial power, are at the same time supposed to be a kind of imitation of the Garden of Eden. Most of all, it must be said that the account of the destruction of the Berlin Zoo, which ought to be too much for the sensibilities of the average reader, probably caused no offense only because it was written by professionals who evidently did not lose their minds even in extremity—or their appetites either, for Heck writes that "the crocodile tails, cooked in large pans, tasted like fat chicken," and later, he continues, "we regarded bear hams and bear sausage as delicacies."[99]

The material in the passages above indicates that attitudes to the realities of a time when urban life in Germany was almost entirely destroyed have been extremely erratic. Leaving aside family reminiscences, sporadic attempts to make literary use of the subject, and the contents of such books of reminiscences as Heck's and Heinroth's, one can speak only of a persistent avoidance of the subject, or an aversion to it. Schäfer's comments on his abandoned project point that way, and so does Wolf Biermann's remark, mentioned by Hage, that he could write a novel about the Hamburg firestorm, in which the clock of his life stopped at six and a half. Neither Schäfer nor Biermann, nor presumably various other people whose clocks also stopped at that time, could bring themselves to go back over their traumatic experiences, for reasons probably to be sought partly in the subject itself, partly in the psychosocial constitution of those affected. In any case, it is difficult to disprove the thesis that we have not yet succeeded in bringing the horrors of the air war to public attention through historical or literary accounts. Typically, those literary works dealing at length with the bombing of the German cities which have been brought to my notice since my Zürich lectures are books that have fallen into obscurity. Otto Erich Kiesel's novel published in 1949 and never reprinted, *Die unverzagte Stadt* ("The Undaunted City")—the title itself makes one uneasy—does not go beyond local historical interest, as Volker Hage says in his article in *Der Spiegel,* and in its whole structure and execution remains below the level on which the German debacle of the last years of the war should be handled. It is more difficult to assess the case of the unjustly forgotten Gert Ledig, who published a novel that attracted much attention, *Die Stalinorgel* ("The Stalin Organ," 1955), and a year later produced another work of some two hundred pages, *Die Vergeltung* ("Retribution"), which went beyond anything Germans were willing to read about their recent past. If *Die Stalinorgel* betrays the influence of the radical antiwar literature of the late Weimar Republic, then *Die Vergeltung,* where in rapid staccato style Ledig traces several different incidents during an hour-long air raid on a nameless city, is a book that attacks the final illusions, and in writing it Ledig was bound to find himself in an offside literary area. It tells of the dreadful end of a group of anti-aircraft auxiliaries barely out of childhood, a priest who has lost his faith, the excesses of a company of soldiers heavily under the influence of alcohol; it deals with rape, murder, and suicide; and it returns again and again to the torments of the human body—teeth and jaws broken, lungs shredded, chests slashed open, skulls burst apart, trickling blood, grotesquely dislocated and crushed limbs, shattered pelvises, people buried under mounds of concrete slabs and still trying to move, waves of detonations, avalanches of rubble, clouds of dust, fire, and smoke. Now and then, printed in italics, there are quieter passages about individuals, obituaries of those whose lives were cut short in this hour of death, each with a few meager facts about his habits, preferences, and wishes. It is not easy to say anything about the quality of this novel. Much of it is written with amazing precision, much else seems awkward and strained. Yet it was certainly not primarily any aesthetic weakness that consigned *Die Vergeltung* and its author, Gert Ledig, to oblivion. Ledig himself must have been a kind of maverick. One of the few reference works to mention him says this: "Born in Leipzig in humble circumstances, and brought up by relations after his mother's suicide, he attended the probationary class of a teacher training college and then studied electrical engineering at a technical college. He volunteered for war service at the age of eighteen, became an officer cadet, but during the Russian campaign found himself in a punishment unit for 'inflammatory talk.' After being wounded for the second time, he was sent on study leave as no longer fit for service at the front, became a shipbuilding engineer, and from 1944 was an industrial expert in the navy. On his way to Leipzig after the war he was arrested by the Russians on suspicion of spying, but escaped from the deportation train. Initially destitute in Munich, he worked as a scaffolder, salesman, and craftsman; for three years from 1950 was an interpreter at the American headquarters in Austria; and was then an engineer with a Salzburg firm. Since 1957 he has lived in Munich as a freelance writer."[100] Even these few facts show that Ledig's background and career did not fit the usual postwar pattern of the life of a man of letters. It is hard to imagine him as a member of Gruppe 47.* His deliberately intense, uncompromising style, designed to evoke disgust and revulsion, once again conjured up the ghost of anarchy at a time when the economic miracle was already on its way; he evoked the fears of general dissolution that threatened the collapse of all order, with humans running wild and descending into lawlessness and irreversible ruin. Ledig's novels, in no way inferior to those of other authors of the 1950s whose names are still known and whose works are discussed, were excluded from cultural memory because they threatened to break through the cordon sanitaire cast by society around the death zones of the dystopian incursions that actually occurred. But these incursions were not solely the product of the machinery of annihilation operating on an industrial scale, in the sense in which Alexander Kluge saw it;

---

*Well-known postwar group of German writers and artists.

they were also the outcome of a myth of decline and destruction propagated increasingly wholeheartedly ever since the rise of Expressionism. The most precise paradigm of that myth is Fritz Lang's 1924 film *Kriemhilds Rache* ("Kriemhild's Revenge"), in which a nation's entire armed forces move forward almost deliberately into the jaws of destruction, finally going up in flames in a stupendous pyromaniacal spectacle. It clearly anticipates the Fascist rhetoric of the "final battle." And while Lang, in Babelsberg, turned Thea von Harbou's visions into images capable of reproduction for German cinema audiences, a decade before Hitler seized power the logisticians of the Wehrmacht were already working on their own Cheruscan* fantasy, a truly terrifying script which provided for the annihilation of the French army on German soil, the devastation of whole areas of the country, and high losses among the civilian population.[101] Even the originator and chief advocate of strategic extremism, General von Stülpnagel, could probably not have envisaged the ultimate outcome of this new battle of the Teutoburger Wald, which left great expanses of the German cities in ruins. Later, our vague feelings of shared guilt prevented anyone, including the writers whose task

---

*Referring to the great Germanic hero Hermann of the Cherusci (Latin: Arminius), who defeated the Romans at the battle of the Teutoburger Wald in A.D. 9.

it was to keep the nation's collective memory alive, from being permitted to remind us of such humiliating images as the incident in the Altmarkt in Dresden, where 6,865 corpses were burned on pyres in February 1945 by an SS detachment which had gained its experience at Treblinka.[102] To this day, any concern with the real scenes of horror during the catastrophe still has an aura of the forbidden about it, even of voyeurism, something that these notes of mine have not entirely been able to avoid. I was not surprised when a teacher in Detmold told me, a little while ago, that as a boy in the immediate postwar years he quite often saw photographs of the corpses lying in the streets after the firestorm brought out from under the counter of a Hamburg secondhand bookshop, to be fingered and examined in a way usually reserved for pornography.

It remains for me, finally, to mention a letter from Darmstadt forwarded to me by the *Neue Zürcher Zeitung*. At the time of writing, this was the last letter about the air war that I had received, and I had to read it several times, because at first I could not believe my eyes. It propounds the theory that the Allies waged war in the air with the aim of cutting off the Germans from their origins and inheritance by destroying their cities, thus paving the way for the cultural invasion and general Americanization that ensued in the postwar period. This deliberate strategy, continues the letter from Darmstadt, was devised by Jews living abroad, exploiting the special knowledge of the human psyche, foreign cultures, and foreign mentalities that they are known to have acquired on their wanderings. The letter, written in a tone as assertive as it is businesslike, closes by hoping that I will reply by sending my professional opinion of the theses it puts forward back to Darmstadt. I do not know who Dr. H., the letter-writer, is, or the nature of his profession, or whether he is involved with some group or party of the radical right, nor can I pronounce on the little cross which he adds to his signature, both handwritten and computer-generated, except that people like Dr. H. who see secret machinations everywhere, working against the vital interests of Germany, like to belong to some kind of order or association. If they are of middle-class origin and so cannot, like the aristocracy, claim to be the natural representatives of the nation's conservative elite, they will range themselves beside the intellectual (and usually self-appointed) defenders of the Christian West or the national heritage. It is well known that the urge to be part of some corporate body which justifies itself by invoking a higher law was particularly strong in the 1920s and 1930s under the conservative and revolutionary right. A line runs straight from George's *Stern des Bundes* to the idea of the coming Reich as the creation of a new league of men, a notion which Alfred Rosenberg propagates in his *Mythus des 20. Jahrhunderts* ("Myth of the 20th Century"), published in the year of grace 1933, and from the first the formation of the SA and SS was intended not only to serve the direct exercise of power but also to attract a new elite bound by unconditional loyalty—a quality that was now also and indeed particularly incumbent on the hereditary nobility. The rivalry between the aristocrats in the Wehrmacht and the new men and career officers who came from lower-middle-class backgrounds, people who like Himmler the amateur chicken breeder now set themselves up as protectors of the Fatherland, is certainly an important chapter in what is as yet the largely unwritten social history of the corruption of the Germans. At what point exactly Dr. H. with his mysterious little cross fits into this picture must be left an open question. Perhaps one could describe him as a revenant from those ill-starred times. So far as I have been able to discover, he is about my age and therefore not of the generation subject to direct Nazi influence. Having made inquiries, I have also discovered that he is not notorious in Darmstadt for being of unsound mind (the one thing that might have been some excuse for his bizarre hypotheses). Indeed, he seems to be in full possession of his mental faculties and obviously lives in respectable circumstances. It is true that the combination of fantastic delusions on the one hand and an upright way of life on the other is typical of the particular fault line that ran through the German mind during the first half of the twentieth century. That fault line is nowhere more evident than in the correspondence between the Nazis, which in its curious mingling of insanity with an alleged interest in objectivity has left a ghostly mark on the ideas set down on paper by Dr. H. As for the actual "theses" that Dr. H. offers, not without pride in his own acumen, they are nothing but a derivative of the so-called "Protocols of the Elders of Zion," that pseudo-documentary forgery first circulated in Tsarist Russia, claiming the existence of an international Jewish body that aimed to dominate the world and ruin entire nations with its conspiratorial wire-pulling. The most virulent variant of this notion was the legend of an enemy, invisible, ever-present, and attacking the nation from within, which was to be found every-where in Germany after the First World War, from the beer table to the press, in the cultural establishment, in the organs of state, and finally reaching the legislature. Whether openly or covertly, that enemy was identified with the Jewish minority. It is obvious that Dr. H. could not take such claims on board without modification, since long before the Allies began their bombing campaign the rhetoric of denunciation had led, throughout the German sphere of influence, to the removal of legal rights from Jews, the confiscation of their property, their exile, and their systematic annihilation. He therefore circumspectly confines his suspicions to Jews living abroad. When, in a curious rider, he contends that those whom he holds re-sponsible for the destruction of Germany acted not so much out of hatred as from their special knowledge of foreign cultures and mentalities, he is crediting them with such motives as those of the subversive genius of self-transformation Dr. Mabuse, in Fritz Lang's film of the same name. Himself of uncertain provenance, Mabuse can adapt to any background. We see him in the first sequence as the speculator Sternberg whose criminal manipulations cause the stock market to crash. As the film goes on he appears as a gambler in illegal casinos, the head of a criminal gang, the power behind a forgery operation, a seditious rabble-rouser and phony revolutionary, and then, under the ominous name of Sandor Weltmann, as a hypnotist with power even over those who do their utmost to withstand him. In a shot characteristically lasting only seconds, the camera shows us, at the front door of this expert operator who can paralyze the will and destroy the mind, a plate with the words: "Dr. Mabuse—Psychoanalyst." Like the foreign Jews of Dr. H.'s imagination, Dr. Mabuse is not motivated by hatred. He is concerned only with power and the desire for power. With his expert understanding of the human psyche, he can get inside the heads of his victims. He ruins the gamblers who play with him, destroys Count Told, steals the Count's wife, and brings his antagonist, the attorney von Wenk, to the brink of death. Von Wenk, who in Thea von Harbou's scenario represents the archetypal Prussian nobleman whom the citizenry trusts to maintain order in times of crisis, finally succeeds in breaking Mabuse's resistance with the help of a contingent from the army (the powers of the police alone proving inadequate), rescuing the Countess and with her, Germany. Fritz Lang's film is a paradigm of the xenophobia that spread among Germans from the end of the nineteenth century onwards. Dr. H.'s remarks about the Jewish specialists in human psychology allegedly behind the strategy of destroying the German cities derive from this hysterical view of German society's constitution as a whole. From a present-day standpoint one may be inclined to dismiss the utterances of Dr. H. as the absurdities of someone who will never learn. And absurd they certainly are, but no less appalling for that. For if anything first set off the immeasurable suffering that we Germans inflicted on the world it was language of this kind, spread out of ignorance and resentment. The majority of Germans today know, or so at least it is to be hoped, that we actually provoked the annihilation of the cities in which we once lived. Scarcely anyone can now doubt that Air Marshal Göring would have wiped out London if his technical resources had allowed him to do so. Speer describes Hitler at a dinner in the Reich Chancellery in 1940 imagining the total destruction of the capital of the British Empire: "Have you ever seen a map of London? It is so densely built that one fire alone would be enough to destroy the whole city, just as it did over two hundred years ago. Göring will start fires all over London, fires everywhere, with countless incendiary bombs of an entirely new type. Thousands of fires. They will unite in one huge blaze over the whole area. Göring has the right idea: high explosives don't work, but we can do it with incendiaries; we can destroy London completely. What will their firemen be able to do once it's really burning?"[103] This intoxicating vision of destruction coincides with the fact that the real pioneering achievements in bomb warfare—Guernica, Warsaw, Belgrade, Rotterdam—were the work of the Germans. And when we think of the nights when the fires raged in Cologne and Hamburg and Dresden, we ought also to remember that as early as August 1942, when the vanguard of the Sixth Army had reached the Volga and not a few were dreaming of settling down after the war on an estate in the cherry orchards beside the quiet Don, the city of Stalingrad, then swollen (like Dresden later) by an influx of refugees, was under assault from twelve hundred bombers, and that during this raid alone, which caused elation among the German troops stationed on the opposite bank, forty thousand people lost their lives.[104]

Between the Devil and the Deep Blue Sea

On Alfred Andersch

IN ALFRED ANDERSCH, GERMAN LITERATURE
HAS DISCOVERED ONE OF ITS SOUNDEST
AND MOST INDIVIDUAL TALENTS.

Alfred Andersch, book jacket text written by himself

THE NOVELIST ALFRED ANDERSCH LACKED NEI-
ther success nor failure in his lifetime. Until 1958,
the year of his "emigration" to Switzerland, he occupied a
key position in the emergent literary world of the Federal
Republic of Germany as a senior editor in radio, initiator
of the influential journal *Texte & Zeichen* ("Texts & Signs"),
and Germany's leading feature writer (as he described
himself to his mother).[1] Later, partly for programmatic
reasons, partly involuntarily, he moved further and further away from the mainstream. On the one hand, con-
cepts of the peripheral, of separation, of withdrawal and
disengagement largely determined the image of himself
developed and circulated by Andersch; on the other, that
image hardly altered the fact that, as the biographical ma-

terial now available shows, he was actually more eager for success and more dependent on it than other prominent authors of the postwar period. It is clear from his letters to his mother that his opinion of his own work was far from restrained. "The Jünger broadcast will be a small sensation"; the play about anti-Semitism on which he claims to be working in 1950 is "the best thing on which I have ever embarked . . . far better than Friedrich Wolf's *Professor Mamlock*";* in Munich, Andersch sees himself "very much the coming man"; his publisher is going to "hold a big reception" at the Frankfurt Book Fair to mark the publication of his novel *Sansibar* ("Zanzibar"), on which, moreover, as he does not fail to inform his mother in the same letter, Professor Muschg, "the most eminent among our literary historians . . . [has] delivered a wonderfully positive verdict." Then Andersch is "in the middle of working on a great radio play," is writing "a great new story," or has "finished a great broadcast." And when *Ein Liebhaber des Halbschattens* ("A Lover of the Half-Shade") is serialized in the *Neue Zürcher Zeitung,* Mama is informed that "this exclusive paper . . . [accepts] only the very best."[2] Such statements are typical not only of the compulsive self-justification governing Andersch's relationship with his mother, but also of his own yearning for

*Wolf was a Communist playwright who raised topical and political issues on the stage during the years of the Weimar Republic.

success and public acclaim, which is in striking contrast to the idea of private, anonymous heroism that, as one of the so-called internal emigrants, he likes to advocate in his books. "Great," in any event, is the operative word in Andersch's assessment and presentation of himself. He wanted to be a great writer writing great works, attending great receptions, and on such occasions casting all the competition as far into the shade as he could, for instance in Milan, "where Mondadori," writes Andersch in an account of his triumph, "gave a reception for me and the French writer Michel Butor" (note the preferential position he accords himself), a reception at which he, Andersch, spoke "for twenty minutes in Italian" and received "thunderous applause," whereas Butor, who then "spoke in French," apparently had to dispense with any applause at all.[3]

The model of the great writer which Andersch adopted from the first in respect of his inner conduct and alignment is acknowledged to have been Ernst Jünger, who had emerged from the Hitler era—which he had helped to usher in—as a distinguished isolationist and defender of humanist values. In point of literary success and fame, Thomas Mann was his outstanding example. The reminiscences of Hans Werner Richter are revealing in this context when he says, of Andersch: "He was ambitious. Not ambitious like other people, no; his ambition went much further. He regarded minor success as perfectly natural and did not pay it any particular attention; he wanted fame, and not just ordinary fame. He thought that could be taken for granted. He aimed to achieve the kind of fame that far outlasted time and space and death, and he would talk about it without inhibition or irony. Once, early on, when the two of us were still editing *Der Ruf** ["The Cry"], he told a large circle of colleagues and friends that he would not only equal Thomas Mann but surpass him. Those present, taken aback, sat there in silence. No one said a word; Fred himself was alone in feeling none of the force of this awkward silence, and probably took it to mean that we agreed with him."[4] And Andersch's grand plan did at first seem to be working out. His autobiographical novel, *Die Kirschen der Freiheit* ("The Cherries of Freedom"), caused much controversy, and not least for that reason was a great success. "Within a very short time," writes Stephan Reinhardt, Andersch's biographer, "the name of Andersch . . . was on all lips in the Federal Republic."[5] As Andersch himself told his boss, Radio Station Intendant Beckmann, he also received letters of approval from "the most notable minds in the country."[6] The string of successes continued with *Sansibar,* which was widely reviewed, with almost unani-

---

*A news sheet representing the views and interests of the "lost generation" who had returned home from the war. It existed for only a brief period in the immediate postwar years before the American occupying authorities, irritated by the editors' arrogance, withdrew its license.

mous praise. Any doubts expressed were qualified, and none of the reviewers noticed the more embarrassing facets of the text. Some even imagined that, through the writing of this novel, the Third Reich had "in the literary sense been overcome."[7] Only when, with the publication of *Die Rote* ("The Redhead"), it became impossible to ignore his conceptual and stylistic weaknesses did the critics split into two camps. Wolfgang Koeppen praised the book as "one of the novels of this century most worth reading,"[8] but Marcel Reich-Ranicki described it as an unappealing mixture of falsehoods and kitsch.[9] Its commercial success—prepublication serialization in the *Frankfurter Allgemeine Zeitung,* high sales figures, promising plans for a film version—allowed Andersch to dismiss adverse reviews at first as the gripes of envious journalists, particularly since Reich-Ranicki did not then exert such great influence as he would a few years later. Largely undeterred, although intent now on a degree of sobriety, Andersch sought to consolidate his claim to fame, as his minor works of the first half of the 1960s show—radio plays, short stories, essays, travelogues. When *Efraim* (translated as "Efraim's Book") finally appeared in 1967, criticism was polarized yet again. Some reviewers praised the book to the skies as a work of "the highest artistic intelligence" and "the novel of the year";[10] others, among them those who really set the tone, no longer minced their words. Rolf Becker, Joachim Kaiser, and Reich-

Ranicki found fault, among other things, with the pretentious style of the novel and used terms such as "kitsch" and "trash." Andersch took so much offense at this unfavorable reception that even two years later, as his biographer tells us, he would not allow "his name to be linked with an exhibition of the 'Kuratorium Unteilbares Deutschland' ["Trustees of Indivisible Germany"] organized by Marcel Reich-Ranicki."[11] "I would consider any association with an exhibition 'organized' by that gentleman defamatory to me," wrote Andersch.[12] A reaction so laden with resentment is hardly surprising in view of the wide gulf between the high literary claims Andersch made for himself and the critical opinion that he was a botcher. That aside, one could hardly take exception to Andersch's angry protests had he not shown himself ready to compromise again at the earliest opportunity. When Reich-Ranicki praised *Mein Verschwinden in Providence* ("My Disappearance in Providence"), for instance, and included a story by Andersch in his anthology *Verteidigung der Zukunft* ("Defense of the Future"), Andersch immediately wrote a conciliatory letter to the critic he so despised, probably not least in hopes of a more favorable reception for his forthcoming major work, the novel *Winterspelt*. But Reich-Ranicki's review of the book in the *Frankfurter Allgemeine Zeitung*, on which Andersch now thought he could count and which appeared four days after the hatchet job Rolf Michaelis did on *Winterspelt* in *Die Zeit* of April 4, 1974, was again very negative, and suggested in the closing sentence that it was hardly worth while going to the trouble of reading it. Andersch took this as the ultimate insult, and his biographer tells us that he thought of suing Reich-Ranicki. "*Winterspelt*," writes Reinhardt, "was to make him famous—and now came this review."[13]

Inevitably, this brief survey of the success and failure of Andersch as a writer raises the question of how we are to understand the opposing views of the critics. Is Andersch one of the most important authors of the postwar decades, as it is now generally assumed in defiance of some of the sharp criticism of his day, or is he not? And if he is not, what was the nature of his failure? Were the flaws in his work merely a matter of occasional stylistic infelicities, or symptoms of a more deep-seated malaise? German academic critics, who unlike the contemporary reviewers in the press found little to object to in Andersch's work, have handled this question with characteristic caution. Accepting the author's declared intentions, they became accomplices in a stratagem of concealment. At least half a dozen monographs on Andersch have now been published, but we have yet to find out what kind of writer he really was. In particular no one (including the critics who took him to task) has tried to cast light on Andersch's compromised stance, strikingly obvious as it is, and on the root causes and effects of such a compromise on literature. It may be appropriate, therefore, to say something here about the decisions Andersch made at various turning points in his life, and the transformation of those decisions in his literary work.

In *Kirschen der Freiheit* an essentially apologetic attitude dominates the urge Andersch sometimes feels for unreserved confession. Memory acts very selectively: decisive tracts of experience are entirely omitted, an editing technique which runs counter to the objectivity announced by the subtitle *Ein Bericht* ("An Account"). The mere three pages in which Andersch describes his three months of imprisonment in Dachau (until May 1933) are strangely cursory and devoid of content. The organization of the text justifies this approach by inserting the passage at the point where Andersch is imprisoned for the second time, in a cell in Munich police headquarters, and thinks back, panic-stricken, to the months he spent in Dachau. It is almost as if he felt barred from calling to mind, either then or later, what he must have seen there. The episode, if one may call it so, of the two Jews Goldstein and Binswanger "shot while trying to escape" ("We heard the sound, like the crack of a whip, while we were sitting on the planks between the huts eating our evening meal"[14]) has something of the character of a Freudian screen memory, allowing the terrible details of what really went on in the camp to be blotted out. But his admission of the fear which seized upon him that afternoon in the police station, making him ready, as he writes, "to say anything required of me,"[15] does bear the mark of authenticity and is one of the most impressive moments in the book, since here Andersch indulges in no posturing. However we evaluate the work, it is clear in these pages at least that Andersch, unlike the great majority of his contemporaries, could entertain no more illusions about the true nature of the Fascist regime. Yet this same immunity from deception in turn casts a highly dubious light on his "internal emigration" during the years that followed.

If we accept Andersch's statement that because of his youth and inexperience "the idea of fleeing abroad"[16] never once entered his head in the time before he was imprisoned, and if we also accept that directly after his release he was in a state of inner paralysis which made him unable to venture on emigration, that still does not explain why he did not take the various opportunities of going to Switzerland offered to him later, between 1935 and 1939. In an interview two years before his death he said openly, for the first time, that he chose the wrong course of action. "I could have emigrated, but I did not. To go into internal emigration under a dictatorship is the worst alternative of all."[17] This confession still does not tell us what induced him to stay. Furthermore, it is doubtful whether Andersch belonged among the internal emigrants in any real sense of the term, even taking into account the fact that membership in that group was not very hard to acquire. There is much to suggest that Andersch's internal emigration was in fact a case of adapting to the prevailing circumstances, a procedure which deeply compromised him. In *Kirschen der Freiheit* he writes of taking refuge in aesthetic pursuits on Sundays and holidays, so that he could "enjoy the rediscovery of my own lost soul in the glaze of Tiepolo's varnishes."[18] On weekdays, the sensitive young man worked "in the accounts department of a publishing firm," and otherwise ignored the society which, as he puts it, "erected the structure of a totalitarian state around me."[19] In view of the fact that Lehmann's Verlagsbuchhandlung in Paul-Heyse-Strasse, where Andersch was employed, was a frontline support agency for the new national policy and concentrated on subjects such as race and racial hygiene, it cannot have been altogether easy to ignore the constant spread of totalitarianism. Stephan Reinhardt is right to describe the house of Lehmann as "the germ cell and breeding ground of racism,"[20] but fails to ask how working for this kind of publisher could be reconciled with an internal emigrant's idea of himself. After all, he could equally well have found a job as a market gardener, and such work might perhaps have been better suited to the increasing need he felt for "immersing myself in nature, for inspiration and new creativity," on which his biographer comments without irony.[21]

The most important omission from the bildungsroman as which Andersch presents *Kirschen der Freiheit* is the story of his marriage to Angelika Albert. Reinhardt tells us that in May 1935 Andersch married Angelika, who was of a German Jewish family, to protect her from the consequences of the Nuremberg Laws, which came into force in September of that year, but also concedes that Angelika's "erotic aura" and her background—the Alberts were an upper-middle-class family of considerable re-pute—may have induced Andersch to contract the mar-riage.[22] The main reason why it is impossible to sustain the argument that Andersch wanted to protect Angelika Albert is that after February 1942, when he was separated from her and from the daughter she had now borne him, he immediately began pressing for a divorce, which he was granted a year later, on March 6, 1943. There is no need to go into more detail about the danger to which Angelika Albert was thus exposed, at a time when mere enforcement of the race laws had long been overtaken by the implementation of the Final Solution. In June 1942 Idl Hamburger, Angelika's mother, had already been "trans-ferred" to Theresienstadt from the Jewish camp at 148 Knorrstrasse in Munich, and she was never to return. Stephan Reinhardt ingenuously comments that Andersch was deeply affected by the circumstances in which he had to sue for divorce, but offers nothing in the way of credi-ble evidence. However, it will strike the impartial reader of Reinhardt's biography that Andersch was principally concerned in that year with giving his life a new direc-tion. He was determined to become a writer, and to that end was assiduously applying for acceptance into the Reichsschrifttumskammer (the Reich Chamber of Literature), membership of which was the prerequisite for any kind of literary publication. Among the various documents required was a certificate of the descent of the applicant's spouse. Andersch sent his application in to the cultural administrator for the Hesse-Nassau region on February 16, 1943, describing himself under the "Marital Status" heading as "divorced" three weeks before his divorce actually came through. Stephan Reinhardt, to whom we owe these grave revelations,[23] dismisses the matter by mentioning an oral communication from Andersch's brother Martin to the effect that Andersch, as mentioned above, was cast into a state of severe moral conflict by his divorce, but on the other hand "his personal development was more important" to him.[24]

It is not easy to make out exactly what this "personal development" was. However, it does seem improbable that Andersch was about to become a Lone Ranger operating for a network of resistance groups, like the young hero Gregor in *Sansibar*. In 1941–42 Germany was at the height of its power, with no end to the Thousand Year Reich in sight. What Andersch wrote at the time, for instance in his story "Der Techniker" ("The Technician"), consequently says a great deal about leadership, blood, instinct, strength, soul, life, the flesh, heritage, health, and race.[25] It is possible to work out from this story, in which

Andersch apparently drew on his experiences with the Albert family, more or less how he might have developed as a writer in the prevailing circumstances. The painter Gisela Groneuer, with whom Andersch was already planning an artistic partnership at the time of his separation from Angelika and who, as Reinhardt writes, brought him "new inspiration,"[26] was urging him to realize his creative potential. In the circumstances, it may not be entirely irrelevant that she was on good terms with local Party functionaries who enabled her to hold three exhibitions in 1943, in Prüm, Luxembourg, and Koblenz. What might have come of the artistic collaboration between Groneuer and Andersch under auspices other than those of the fall of the Third Reich is a question that must remain open. As a postscript to this story of German-Jewish and German-German parting and pairing off, however, it may be added that on October 8, 1944, when he was a POW, Alfred Andersch petitioned the authorities of Camp Ruston, Louisiana, for the return of his confiscated papers and manuscripts. The main gist of his submission runs as follows: "Prevented from free writing, up to now, my wife being a mongrel of jewish [sic] descent . . . and by my own detention in a German concentration-camp for some time, these papers and diaries contain the greatest part of my thoughts and plans collected in the long years of oppression."[27] The shocking aspect of this document is the man's aggressive self-righteousness, the horrible descrip-

To the Authorities of the PoW-Camp Ruston / La.

8. 10. 1944

Dear Sirs,

I beg to submit to you the following entreaty:
Upon my arrival on board the steamer "Samuel Moody" at
Norfolk /USA. from Naples (29.8.1944) my diaries, letters
and the manuscript of a narrative were taken from me
for censorship with the remark that all these things
would be returned to me as soon as possible. The papers
were put into a brown envelope bearing my name
and PoW-Number. Being a writer, all these things are
most valuable and irretrievable to me. Prevented
from free writing, up to now, my wife being a mongrel
of jewish descent, and by my own detention in a
German concentration-camp for some time, these papers
and diaries contain the greatest part of my thoughts
and plans collected in the long years of opression.
I therefore beg you most urgently to restore them to
me at the earliest possible convenience. I also beg to

tion of Angelika as "a mongrel of jewish descent"——in
terms deriving one way or another from the warped notions of racist ideology——and above all the fact that
Andersch does not now shrink from reclaiming Angelika
as "my wife," despite their divorce some time earlier, and

inform you that your intelligence officers behind the
Italian front perused these notes and gave them back to
me again. Even a major who spoke to me in an exami-
nation-camp near Washington two weeks ago promised
to see that my diaries etc. would be returned to me as
soon as possible.

Hoping that you will comply with my request and
thanking you in advance for your kind intervention
I remain

very respectfully
yours
ALFRED ANDERSCH
PW-No.: 81 G 256 993

after he had concealed her existence in his application to
the Reich Chamber of Literature. He could hardly have
devised a shabbier trick.

The second part of *Kirschen der Freiheit* is almost exclusively concerned with Andersch's military career and its

end when he deserted. In his account of it, Andersch is first called up in 1940 to join a guards battalion in Rastatt. Soon he is stationed on the Upper Rhine, looking across to France on the other bank. With unusual frankness, of a kind which unfortunately bore no more fruit in his work, he writes that at the time he "did not even want to desert. I had sunk so low that I thought a German victory possible."[28] There cannot have been many reasons for Andersch to change his mind over the next two years. Indeed, his opinion must have been reinforced as it became increasingly obvious that Germany was now unassailable. Nothing will have been further from Andersch's mind at the time than the idea of resistance, and one cannot rule out a certain degree of opportunistic identification with the successful regime. Martin Andersch probably had a good point in speaking, as Reinhardt discreetly comments in a footnote, of a "phase of instability" in his brother's career.[29] Andersch's success in returning to civilian life in the spring of 1941, by dint of referring to his detention in a concentration camp, can hardly be regarded as an act of resistance,[30] any more than he can be blamed for feeling no ardent wish to go to the front line. When he received his second call-up in 1943 he wrote to his mother saying he would try to get a post as a reserve officer.[31] Later he applied for a cushy job in the Air Ministry. On the other hand, he resents the fact that the reserve company to which he was assigned consisted almost entirely of dodgers.[32] What Andersch's true views were at that point is not easily ascertained. In any case, he can be said to have been pleasantly surprised when, despite his own evasive efforts, he was sent to war. He told his mother at home that he had been riding on a motorbike with his superior officer through the sunny south. "Pisa, the Leaning Tower, the cathedral and . . . a wonderful Italian landscape with beautiful façades looking out on the Arno rushed past me. We are billeted in a lovely little village . . . the evening is mild and warm, the Chianti bottle goes round. And for all this one must still be 100% the soldier. But it's fun."[33] This is his real voice at the time, and it helps us to assess the degree of veracity in *Kirschen der Freiheit*. It gives a more accurate idea of the history of Alfred Andersch's development than does the literary work he made of it. Wartime tourism prepared the way for later travels, and Andersch was not the only middle-class German citizen to feel a certain elation in the experience. "It's amazing," he wrote home from Louisiana in December 1944, "to think of all I've seen this year."[34] Set against this background, his elaborate account of his desertion as a statement of existential self-determination loses something of its Hemingway-like luster, and Andersch appears simply—although it can hardly be held against him—a man who made off into the bushes when a good opportunity arose.

In the years after the war Andersch first came into the public eye as editor and leader-writer of the journal *Der*

Ruf, a debut which was scarcely less compromised than his previous more or less private history. In 1966, in a chapter of some thirty pages in a dissertation published under a West German imprint and entitled *1945 oder die "neue Sprache"* ("1945, or the 'New Language' "), Urs Widmer cites much evidence to show that the articles written by Richter and Andersch derive their inspiration almost without exception from the period before 1945.[35] Not that the evidence was difficult to find, for *Der Ruf* is a positive glossary and index of Fascist language. When Andersch writes in the first issue (August 1946) that "the youth of Europe . . . will campaign with fanatical zeal against all enemies of freedom,"[36] he is merely producing a variation on the New Year message of 1944 in which Hitler announced his determination to conduct the approaching decisive battle "with the utmost fanaticism and to its ultimate conclusion."[37] This is not the place to dilate on the material that could be cited to this effect from almost every part of Andersch's articles; however, it may be said that linguistic corruption and an addiction to empty, spiraling pathos are only the outward symptoms of a warped state of mind which is also reflected in the content of his pieces. The amazing presumptuousness with which Andersch, who all things considered had had quite a comfortable war, now elected himself spokesman for "those who fought at Stalingrad, El Alamein and Cassino," and whom, in his comments on the Nuremberg Trials, he

absolves of any share of the blame for the crimes committed at Dachau and Buchenwald, [38] is not an isolated lapse;
rather, this contribution, made with unconcealed fervor,
to the myth, just arising at the time, of the collective innocence of the Wehrmacht is very much in line with the
positions generally defended in *Der Ruf.* We may also
note that Andersch, who usually paid very close attention
to everything written about him, obviously overlooked
Widmer's book. At least, there is no reference to it in
Reinhardt's carefully researched biography. Specialist
monographs on Andersch (for instance by Volker Wehdeking and Erhard Schütz) also fail to mention the thesis
put forward by Widmer, which is a rather awkward one
for the neutralizing operations regularly performed in the
field of Germanist studies. Andersch himself indirectly
acknowledges Widmer only thirteen years later, when
Fritz J. Raddatz mentions Andersch and Widmer's work
at the beginning of his essay "Wir werden weiterdichten,
wenn alles in Scherben fällt . . ." ("We Will Continue to
Write When Everything Falls Apart . . ."), published
by *Die Zeit* on April 12, 1979. In a statement also printed
in *Die Zeit*, Andersch—to his credit, be it said—unreservedly agrees with Raddatz's remarks. It is hard to
say what impelled him to make this gesture. The lavish
praise which Andersch heaps on the writer of this piece
sounds to me a little suspect. "I cannot remember," he
says, "when I last read an essay on literary politics of such

brilliance and cogency. A phenomenal study." He is also overdoing it slightly when he comments: "I agree entirely . . . particularly in those passages which are critical of me. Today I go much further than Raddatz in criticizing many remarks I made in my early period (and not then alone)." As far as I know there is no evidence to back up this claim, which swiftly closes the unpleasant subject again, unless we assume it to be the offer made by Andersch in the same place to withdraw his essay on Thomas Mann, which he now finds he does not like at all. However, one could see Andersch's response to Raddatz as a late confession and a sign that at this time—a few months before his death, when he was very much in extremis—he may have looked back on his life's work with a certain sense of remorse.

Andersch's first real novel after the autobiographical *Kirschen der Freiheit* was his book *Sansibar oder der letzte Grund* ("Zanzibar, or the Last Reason"), although on closer study this too proves to be a piece of fictionalized autobiography, covering what was left out of *Kirschen der Freiheit*. Of the characters in this work, the central couple (Gregor and Judith) undoubtedly correspond to the real Alfred Andersch and Angelika Albert. The difference lies in the fact that Andersch makes Gregor the secret hero he never was himself, and that Judith is not abandoned but rescued by Gregor and taken into exile, even though she is "a spoiled girl from a rich Jewish family"[39] who does not deserve it. Few emotions are harder to repress than resentment. Moreover, Judith is identified as Jewish the moment she first appears in Rerik: "A Jewess, thought Gregor, she's a Jewess, what's she doing here in Rerik? . . . Gregor recognized the face at once: it was one of those young Jewish faces of a kind he had often seen at the Youth Association in Berlin or Moscow. This was a particularly fine specimen [!! WGS] of such a face."[40] And a few pages further on, Judith is again portrayed as "a black-haired young girl . . . with a beautiful, tender, and alien face showing the features of her race [!! WGS] . . . hair flowing over a pale, elegantly cut trench coat."[41] As befits a Jewish girl, Judith exerts a special erotic attraction. No wonder that Gregor's senses begin to whirl, in a chiaroscuro scene typical of Andersch. "He went very close to her and put his left arm around her shoulders. Now the general impression of her face was lost, he could not make out her eyes, but instead he felt the fragrance of her skin, her nose slipped past him [!! WGS], her cheeks, and finally there was only her mouth, her mouth—still dark, but with a lovely curving line, it wavered close [!! WGS] and then dissolved."[42] At this point, to save Gregor from forgetting the gravity of the situation entirely and allow him to get control of himself just in time, Andersch makes the church door open with a creak. "When the light of the torch fell in, he was already two paces away from Judith."[43] Gregor's political disengagement is central to the narrative of *Sansibar,* along with the frustrated love story. The young hero's moment of truth had come a few years earlier, when he was taking part as a guest in a Red Army military exercise: "He had seen the town lying there at the foot of the hill in the steppes, a jumble of gray huts on the shores of a melting golden sea . . . and Comrade Lieutenant Kholchov had called to him: That's Tarasovka, Grigoriy! We've taken Tarasovka! Gregor smiled back, but he did not care whether or not the tank brigade [. . .] had taken Tarasovka, he was suddenly fascinated by the molten gold of the waters of the Black Sea and the gray of the huts along the banks, a dirty silver plumage which seemed to draw itself together before the threat of fifty tanks fanning out in formation, moving with a sound like a hollow drone, fifty resonant clouds of the dust of the steppes, fifty arrows of iron dust against which Tarasovka raised the golden shield of its sea."[44] We may assume the subject of this lavish word-painting to be the way the beauty of the world dawns on the eyes of a man hitherto blind to it. We must further conclude that such an overwhelming experience is to be equated in the textual system with the revelation of a higher truth repudiating the hero's previous life (in this case, his political commitment). It would be foolish to deny that such epiphanies have proved valid in works of literature. But it is one thing for the words really to take off, another for them to be tastelessly overloaded, as in this much-cited passage, with recherché adjectives, nuances of literary color, a tinselly glitter, and other cheap ornaments. When a morally compromised author claims the field of aesthetics as a value-free area it should make his readers stop and think. The burning of Paris was, for Ernst Jünger, a wonderful sight! Frankfurt burning, as seen from the Main, is for Andersch "a terrifyingly beautiful image."[45] There is a passage in *Kirschen der Freiheit* which has nothing to do with the narrative in itself but in which, as if incidentally, the shape of a new aesthetic is traced, in apparently diametrical opposition to the aesthetic Andersch despised "of pretentiously stylized Symbolist writers and painters."[46] A certain Dick Barnett is cited as its advocate. He sits, according to Andersch, in an office of the Lockheed Aircraft Corporation in Burbank, California, "drawing"—try imagining it—"the outlines of the F94 jet fighter." "He does this primarily in obedience to careful calculations, that is to say with the help of his reason, but only passion can create so pure a form, a form in which the secret struggle between courage and fear still quivers in Dick Barnett's breast, making us aware that when Barnett created it he was balancing on a knife edge. One small deviation and he would have fallen. A single wrong turn of Barnett's mind—and the F94 jet fighter would not have been the perfect work of art it is. And unknown to Barnett, the atmosphere of Burbank, California, has played its part, the particular shade of red of the fuel pumps at a filling station seen in the morning on the way to the Lockheed works, the line of his wife's throat under a streetlight when they left the car yesterday evening coming home from the cinema."[47] This, then, is Andersch's vision of a new New Objectivity, an art taking as its principle the association of aesthetics with technology, with politics (or to be precise political defeatism), and ultimately with violence and war. The model for this elaborate passage on the creation of pure form was probably Ernst Jünger's concept of armed virility. The conjecture, both romantic and questionable, that Barnett owes his creative power to certain moods induced, say, by the line of his wife's throat as seen under a streetlight, shows that conversely it was bound to be very difficult for a disciple of Jünger to represent femininity in literary terms.

Andersch would probably have been well advised to exercise self-restraint in this respect, like the master himself, for he bares his soul to us only too clearly in the set pieces which occur in all his books describing the female body. In this respect, he scales the heights of humbug in his novel of the late 1950s, *Die Rote,* which as usual employs two distinct models of representation. In particularly emotional passages the female face is regularly depicted as if it were an advertisement for shampoo or Coca-Cola: hair blowing in the wind is its unmistakable trademark. The Mouson Lavendel advertising man Andersch once was patently knows the knack of it. For instance: "at the moment when she stepped out of the niche the wind streamed through her hair, sweeping it smoothly back with a single movement to form a shallow wave of dark red. And it was the form of this wave, falling slightly from the top of her head to rise again and end in a tangle of radiant color like spray, spray from the wave of a dark red sea, it was the uncontrollable soft, laconic movement of this wave of dark Pompeian red that finally fanned out, not darkly black but only shot through with black, with the color of coal, subsiding slightly now, shining only in the translucent web of its edges, it was this movement of a particle of the tide of a Pompeian sea caught spellbound like a sign or signal against a background of the purest azure that the skies above Venice could offer—it was this that penetrated Fabio's optic nerves like the verse of a poem."[48] Andersch gave his Venetian novel an epigraph from Monteverdi. It runs: "The modern composer writes his works by constructing them on a foundation of truth." But anyone taking the trouble to work out the relationship between truth and composition in the lines quoted would certainly conclude that falsification has replaced the former and a tortuous Pompeian pretentiousness the latter. No less trashy, besides being lascivious in an extremely unpleasant manner, are Andersch's stereotyped depictions of physical intimacy, which follow this kind of pattern: "She embraced and kissed him; when her arms were round his neck he felt her tender, scintillating physical warmth, the thin and radiant film tracing the contours of her shoulders, her arms, her bosom more insistently than did the faint fragrance of her perfume and the black and white silk of her nightdress and negligee. She was as small and slim as her sister, but while Celia was merely slender, Giulietta was almost thin. Thin and electric."[49] The ingredients employed here—scintillating body warmth, fragrant perfume, the contours of the shoulders, the radiant film (we are not told exactly what it is), the unfortunate word "bosom"—unite into the confused wishful thinking of a voyeur invisibly participating, as the omniscient author—she embraces him, he feels her warmth—in the scene he has staged for his own gratification. The fact that in addition to containing such embarrassing passages the novel *Die Rote* takes Germany's notorious past as its subject, using Auschwitz as a kind of background to set the scene, reinforces the obscenity of this hopelessly misconceived piece of literature. Various attempts have been made to salvage *Die Rote* by arguing that those German critics who attacked the book did not understand the genre novels of the English-speaking world and their way of creating suspense, or the lively atmosphere of Italian neorealism adopted by Andersch here.[50] One can only say first that Alfred Andersch's Venetian kitsch and the garden of the Finzi-Contini are light-years apart, and second that genre literature, which at its best can undoubtedly satisfy high literary claims, should not be cited in defense of a novel which makes high literary claims for itself and then drops into the depths of banality.

Efraim was an ambitious project from the first, and Andersch hoped that it would finally secure him a place in the first rank of German novelists. Work on the book lasted for several years—for one reason, probably because Andersch wanted to ensure that the flaws pointed out by critics in his last novel did not creep in again. Indeed, the reader does initially gain an impression that this is a more serious and more solidly constructed work, but that impression will not stand up to closer examination. The subject of *Efraim* is the return of an English journalist of German Jewish origin to his native city of Berlin after almost a quarter of a century to make inquiries about the missing Esther, daughter of his boss and colleague Keir Horne. The story of the lost daughter (who was betrayed, as Efraim makes clear to us, by her father) is sidelined, so to speak, in the structure of the text, and depicted in a way which, paradoxically, allows the author to ignore the fact that in her he is touching on the trauma of his own moral failure. There are no links enabling one to identify the fictional figure of Keir Horne with Andersch the author of the book. Far from recognizing his alter ego in Keir Horne, who "[must] have fathered Esther in 1925 when he went off with one of the most beautiful women in the Berlin of that time,"[51] he chooses

George Efraim to represent him. More precisely, he puts himself into the character, ruthlessly taking him over, until the reader gradually comes to realize that there is no George Efraim anymore, only an author maneuvering in place of his victim. The evidence for this claim lies in the linguistic style of the novel, which consists entirely of the notes of George Efraim. Efraim writes in his mother tongue of German, which he has to dredge up from far away in the dark past. However, although he expressly mentions the rediscovery of his native language several times in the novel, there is no sense in the text itself of the difficult and painful archaeological labor that in real life it surely would have entailed; to one's considerable surprise, and entirely *sans gêne,* George Efraim is perfectly at ease with contemporary German jargon, speaking of a character "der nicht plötzlich zu rotieren beginnt" ("who does not suddenly get into a flap") when a woman leaves him, or wondering "ob er seiner Begleiterin nicht mächtig auf den Wecker fällt" ("whether he is not getting on his female companion's wick").[52] Examples of such primitive idiomatic turns of phrase, the tediousness of which is not easily conveyed in translation, could be multiplied. There is no trace in the text of any linguistic scruples on the part of either protagonist or author. Now and then, however, it must have occurred to Andersch that he had not hit upon entirely the right tone for George Efraim, since on occasion—prophylactically, so to speak—he makes him mention the fact that he is easily seduced into the speech patterns employed by his former countrymen.[53] Such rationalizations, however, are reminiscent of the story of silly Kate who tips good wheat flour into the spilt beer. In the circumstances, the key scene of the novel is thoroughly implausible. Efraim finds himself at a party with Anna when he overhears someone he has never met before saying that he intends to go on making merry "bis zur Vergasung" ("until I'm gassed"), a particularly notorious German phrase, still quite prevalent in the postwar years, which must have entered the popular vocabulary in the 1940s. "I went up to him," writes Efraim/Andersch, "and asked: 'What did you say?' Then, without waiting for an answer, I came in with an uppercut [!! WGS]. Though he was a head taller than I, he was not exactly the athletic type, and I had learned the rudiments of boxing in the army."[54] What is so particularly irritating in this scene is not just the yobbish drift of the narrative and the way in which Andersch attempts to ward off any objections in advance, but most of all the fact that it removes any shred of credibility from the narrator Efraim and his creator. Efraim's violent outburst, intended to reflect legitimate moral outrage, really shows that Andersch is involuntarily projecting into the mind of his Jewish protagonist a German soldier showing a Jew how best to deal with his own kind. In the subtext of this scene the roles are therefore reversed. I should add here that Andersch is known to have taken a great deal of trouble over his research into the Jewish background for this book, and even, as Reinhardt faithfully reports, offered "Dr. Ernst Ludwig Ehrlich of Basel, the authority on Judaism," a fee "to look through the Jewish parts of the novel."[55] Despite these earnest efforts, Jewish readers—not only Reich-Ranicki but also Edmund Wolf of London, Andersch's acquaintance of many years—could see nothing Jewish in Efraim, which surprises me as little as the information, also imparted by Reinhardt, that Andersch was offended when Edmund Wolf wrote to him saying so.

Finally, *Winterspelt*—the Eifel in the snow, a few figures in an empty landscape, armies temporarily immobilized, crows in flight, a sinister silence: the time is just before the Ardennes offensive. The book is written thoughtfully, with more care and circumspection than any of Andersch's other novels; it unfolds slowly, the perspective changing frequently, and the documentary context gives the whole work something of an objective note. It is certainly Andersch's best book, yet it is still an apologia. It deals with plans for a Resistance operation. The protagonist is Major Joseph Dincklage ("After 1938 a variety of military academies; at the outbreak of war, officer candidate; by spring of 1940, second lieutenant [Upper Rhine Front]; 1941–42, first lieutenant and captain [Africa]; 1943, Knights' Cross and promotion to major [Sicily]; from autumn 1943 to autumn 1944 with the occupation forces in

Paris and Denmark").[56] Major Dincklage has for some time been intending to surrender his battalion to the Americans. Käthe Lenk, a right-minded schoolmistress who admires Dincklage for his Knights' Cross—"although she hated the war"[57]—is in on the secret plan. One may assume that these two fictional figures represent Alfred and Gisela Andersch, who also became close to each other in the Eifel although under rather different circumstances: that is to say, it is rather unlikely that they ever discussed the possibility of resistance together. At that point, after all, no one could know how the war would turn out. Käthe and Dincklage are figments of retrospective wishful thinking; Andersch would have liked himself and Gisela to resemble the couple in the novel, if not necessarily at the time then at least after the event. This is literature as a means of straightening out one's own past life. Käthe's instinctive honesty makes her the ideally incorruptible character. Her soul is proof against the evil regime. Dincklage, too, is above suspicion. Like Jünger, also a recipient of the Knights' Cross, he survives the wintry season in the army with decency and composure, and is now about to draw his own conclusions from a fundamentally hopeless situation. "The question of courage is one that does indeed concern an officer."[58] Consequently a man like Dincklage must try to start a move towards wholesale desertion. Simply withdrawing like any other soldier is not an option open to him, and it is not Dincklage's fault that ultimately his plan fails. The messenger Schefold is shot in no-man's-land between the fronts by the brutal soldier Reidel, who as it happens is easily the most credible figure in the whole novel. Andersch knows Reidel's language. By comparison, Dincklage is a cardboard cutout. He is a difficult character, is introduced—rather like the heroic Pastor Helander who dies with his boots on in *Sansibar,* meeting the Gestapo with a revolver—as a sufferer from physical pain (coxarthrosis and a war wound), and is also an existentialist plagued by high-minded doubts, walking on a knife edge in a borderline situation. German existentialism as personified in Dincklage, however, unlike its French equivalent, lacks the justification of organized resistance and ultimately remains an empty, false gesture, fictional, private, gratuitous. In *Winterspelt,* as in the earlier *Sansibar,* Andersch converts the attempt of the internal emigrants to compensate for this moral deficit, through the symbolic representation of resistance in art, into a fable suggesting that condemned works of art were salvaged and moved into exile. Whether such retrospective fictions add up to an aesthetic of resistance seems to me doubtful.

One last brief word. Much has been said of Andersch's return to the left towards the end of his life, mainly because of the controversy he unleashed in the year 1976 with his poem "Artikel 3(3)" on the subject of official debarment from certain professions, in which he claimed that new concentration camps were already in existence.

It may have been necessary for someone to overstate the facts slightly, but nonetheless this notorious affair, which has entered the canon of literary history, gives rise to a certain sense of disquiet because of the rather abrupt way in which Andersch assumed such an unreservedly radical attitude. He had certainly always liked to suggest that his exile in the canton of Ticino in Switzerland was forced upon him by intolerable conditions in Germany, but no one ever took him seriously. What I consider really characteristic of Andersch and his attitude to Germany and its political constitution is his comment, in a letter to his friend Wolfgang Weyrauch in Hamburg in 1959: "I watch, with a malicious grin . . . as you all stew in your own neo-Nazi juices and have to reconstruct resistance movements. It's a fine thing to be behind the lines. . . ."[59] At heart, Andersch was always a man who stayed behind the lines himself. It was therefore only natural for him to become a Swiss citizen in the early 1970s, although there was no pressing need for him to take such a step. There is anecdotal evidence, related by Reinhardt, that Andersch thought he could rely on the good offices of his neighbor, the writer Max Frisch, to support his application for Swiss naturalization. According to Reinhardt, Andersch was sorely disappointed, and indeed felt defamed, when he learned that Frisch had written: "He values Switzerland, but Switzerland is not one of his preoccupations."[60] Andersch's self-centered reaction to this insufficiently glowing reference offers a final insight into a mental existence plagued by ambition, egotism, resentment, and rancor. His literary work is the cloak in which those qualities wrap themselves, but its lining, which is less attractive, keeps showing through.

Against the Irreversible

On Jean Améry

A RUSTLING AND CRACKLING AND HISSING.
WHAT WAS IT THEY SAID? BE CAREFUL OR
YOU WILL BURN, ALL ABLAZE. ALL A BLAZE.
LET MY UNHAPPINESS BURN AND BE
EXTINGUISHED IN THE FLAMES.

Jean Améry, Lefeu oder der Abbruch
("Lefeu, or Demolition")

IN THE MID-SIXTIES, WHEN AFTER A LONG SI-lence Jean Améry came before the public of the German-speaking world again with his essays on exile, resistance, torture, and genocide, the literary figures of the new Federal Republic (of which he was rather wary) were anxious to compensate for the huge moral deficit which, until about 1960, had been a feature of the literature of the postwar period. It is not easy to form an idea of the barriers Améry had to surmount when he decided to enter into the debate then beginning. The fact that experiences such as his own were no longer taboo in public discourse must have helped him to define his own position; on the other hand, his task was made more difficult by the very circumstance that so few authentic voices had been raised in that debate, although it did at least represent progress by comparison with the extraordinary indifference of the 1950s. In many ways, however, the alacrity with which literature was now reclaiming "Auschwitz" as its own territory was no less repellent than its previous refusal to broach that monstrous subject at all. The astonishing efficacy with which moral capital was now being made from denunciation of the collective amnesia encouraged by the literary world itself could easily cast the wrong light on a man who, like Jean Améry, had really suffered, yet again pointing up his difference from all who were now contributing their own mite of accusation, although their change of attitude to the dreadful chapter of events now becoming past history did not otherwise affect their quality of life. In fact, only a few authors, for instance Peter Weiss, managed to find the requisite gravity of language for the subject and make the literary treatment of genocide more than a dutiful exercise marked by involuntary infelicities. But the accounts of the Final Solution written in the sixties, where a generalized dramatic and poetic tone often obstructed closer understanding of those terrible events, should not be simply dismissed with this argument. For all their ethical and aesthetic inadequacies, they do constitute the first step in an attempt to reveal the truth through literary efforts; these efforts are still in progress, and have now come to present far more relevant and subtly differentiated views.

From the first, the unique position of Améry's writings in this context rested on the fact that he had not become aware of the realities of genocide merely through historical and juridical analysis; for two and a half decades he had himself been literally occupied with the destruction inflicted on him and those like him. Rather than being abstract accounts of the victims of National Socialism, accounts which only too easily acknowledged a monstrous liability, the essays written by Améry at this time about his personal past and present contain insights, based on the most direct experience, into the irreparable condition of those victims, and it is from such insights alone that the true nature of the terror visited on them can be extrapolated with some precision. It is part of the psychic and social condition of the victim that he cannot receive compensation for what was done to him. History is still working through that condition, and so above all is the principle of brute force behind it. Once a victim, always a victim. "Twenty-two years later," writes Améry, "I am still dangling over the ground by dislocated arms."[1] The affective equivalent of this condition, which remains unresolved despite all attempts at jurisdiction and compensation, is silence, as Améry well knew. What raised Améry's work above the literary activity surrounding it was the way in which he tried to break through the silence imposed on him by terrorism, in the face of a situation where those who came after the Fascist regime, and were at most only indirectly affected themselves, were usurping the victims' cause. Améry's contribution to the discussion was far from conciliatory. He insistently points out that the persecution and extermination of a largely assimilated minority, as planned and put into practice in the German Reich, is "singular and irreducible" in the very fact of its "total inner logic and appalling rationality,"[2] and that in the last resort the question is not so much one of constructing a plausible etiology of terror as of achieving some ultimate understanding of what it means to be marked out as a victim, excluded, persecuted, and murdered.

In considering the essays written by Jean Améry in the fourteen years between 1960 and his death, one notices both their almost exclusively autobiographical approach and their relatively slight narrative content. The reflective tendency characteristic of Améry's work must certainly have been predetermined by the essay form on which he had decided; on the other hand, there is also undeniable evidence of his need to depict the course and outcome of events in his own life, a need which, out of reluctance and the fear of facing what had happened and what was still to come, he often expressed only in qualified or very restrained terms. Améry's accounts of his origins, childhood, and youth, his *Unmeisterliche Wanderjahre* (as the title of one of his works runs, alluding to Goethe's *Wilhelm Meisters Lehrjahre*) are as sparing in concrete detail as what he says about his Resistance work and his survival in Auschwitz. It is as if every fragment of memory touched a sore point, as if he were compelled to ward off everything immediately and translate it into reflective form to make it at all measurable by any standard. The fact that memory can hardly be endured—memory not only of moments of terror but also of a more or less untroubled time before them—is a problem which to a high degree determines the mental state of victims of persecution. The psychoanalyst William Niederland has referred to the fact that they try, usually in vain and at great expense of energy, to banish what has happened to them from their minds.[3] Unlike the agents of terror, they obviously no longer have reliable mechanisms of repression at their command. Islands of amnesia do develop in them, but that is not at all the same as being genuinely able to forget. Rather, it is as if a diffuse ability to forget goes hand in hand with the recurrent resurgence of images that cannot be banished from the memory, and that remain effective as agencies of an almost pathological hypermnesia in a past otherwise emptied of content. The anguish of memory which is partly vague, partly full of a still acute fear of death, can be traced in Améry's writings. How much more unreal, further in the past, and harder for him to remember than the mere passage of time would justify was his childhood in Ischl and Gmunden; how much closer and more enduring must the days in July of 1943 when he was tortured by the

Gestapo in Fort Breendonk always have seemed. The gathering and mental organization of experiences is usually determined by the emotional states associated with them, and does not shatter the diachronic framework. For the victims of persecution, however, the thread of chronological time is broken, background and foreground merge. the victim's logical means of support in his existence are suspended. The experience of terror also dislocates time, that most abstract of all humanity's homes. The only fixed points are traumatic scenes recurring with a painful clarity of memory and vision. Améry will certainly have been exposed to this distressing dynamic during his years of silence, when he earned a living as a journalist but wrote nothing about his own life. At any rate, he expressly says in his preface to *Jenseits von Schuld und Sühne* ("Beyond Guilt and Atonement," translated into English under the title *At the Mind's Limits*), "I cannot say that during the time I was silent I had forgotten or 'repressed' the twelve years of German fate, or of my own. For two decades I had been in search of the time that was impossible to lose, but it had been difficult for me to talk about it."[4] The paradox of searching for a time which, to the author's own distress, cannot in the last resort be forgotten entails the quest for a form of language in which experiences paralyzing the power of articulation could be expressed. Améry found it in the open method of the essay genre, where he conveyed both the damaged emotions of a man brought to the brink of death and the supremacy of a mind intent on thinking freely even in extremis, however useless doing so might seem. Through the effort he expended on this enterprise he succeeded, within what he himself knew better than anyone would be the very short time left to him, in reconstructing his memory to the point where it became accessible to him and to us.

His memoirs could not, of course, be a narrative in any traditional sense, and they therefore dispense with any kind of literary stylization which might encourage a sense of complicity between the writer and his readers. Améry employs a pervasive strategy of understatement which prohibits both pity and self-pity, and according to Niederland's findings is typical of all the accounts of victims of persecution. Even Améry's description of his torture is in a tone emphasizing the monumental madness of the procedure inflicted on him rather than the emotional aspect of his suffering.

In the bunker there hung from the vaulted ceiling a chain that above ran into a roll. At its bottom end it bore a heavy, broadly curved iron hook. I was led to the instrument. The hook gripped into the shackle that held my hands together behind my back. Then I was raised with the chain until I hung about a metre above the floor. In such a position, or rather, when hanging this way, with your hands behind your back, for a short time you can hold at a half-oblique through muscular force. During these few minutes, when you are already expending your utmost strength, when sweat has already appeared on your forehead and lips, and you are breathing in gasps, you will not answer any questions. Accomplices? Addresses? Meeting places? You hardly hear it. All your life is gathered in a single, limited area of the body, the shoulder joints, and it does not react; for it exhausts itself completely in the expenditure of energy. But this cannot last long, even with people who have a strong physical constitution. As for me, I had to give up rather quickly. And now there was a cracking and splintering in my shoulders that my body has not forgotten to this hour. The balls sprang from their sockets. My own body weight caused luxation; I fell into a void and now hung by my dislocated arms which had been torn high from behind and were now twisted over my head. Torture, from Latin *torquere,* to twist. What visual instruction in etymology![5]

The phrase with which this curiously objective passage concludes, provocatively deviating almost into the ridiculous, shows that the composure, the *impassibilité* allowing Améry to recapitulate such extreme experiences has here reached breaking point. Améry resorts to irony where otherwise his voice would be bound to falter. He knows that he is operating on the borders of what language can convey. "If someone wanted to impart his physical pain," he writes, "he would be forced to inflict it and thereby become a torturer himself."[6] He can therefore only reflect in the abstract on the total "transformation of the person into flesh" in torture, pain being "the most extreme intensification imaginable of our bodily being."[7] Améry describes extremes of torture and the pain they cause as an approach to the death to which otherwise "no road that can be travelled by logic" leads. This is the knowledge from which he sets out, as a man who will carry death within him ever after. Torture, writes Améry, has "an indelible character. Whoever was tortured, stays tortured."[8] This is the lapidary revelation which he presents to us without the slightest attempt to emotionalize his case.

It is this scrupulous restraint in his account of the torture he suffered that enables Améry to put forward a theory about what he still regards as the dark riddle of Nazi Fascism, one in which the common explanation of it as a national perversion has no place. He sees the practice of persecuting, torturing, and exterminating an arbitrarily chosen adversary not as a lamentable but incidental feature of totalitarian rule but, unreservedly, as its essential expression. He remembers "serious, tense faces [. . .] concentrated in murderous self-realization. With heart and soul they went about their business, and the name of it was power, domination over spirit and flesh, an orgy of unchecked self-expansion."[9] To Améry, the world devised and realized by German Fascism was the world of torture in which "man exists only by ruining the other person who stands before him."[10] Améry's train of thought leads him to Georges Bataille. The radical position he thus assumes excludes any compromise with history, and here lies the specific importance of Améry's work in the context of literary approaches to the German past, which in one way or another had always shown a certain readiness to compromise. There were no uncompromisingly negative thinkers such as Bataille or Cioran in postwar German literature, and Améry is still the only one who denounced the obscenity of a psychologically and socially deformed society, and the outrage of supposing that history could proceed on its way afterwards almost undisturbed, as if nothing had happened. Améry, who was liable to the death threat inherent in the Nuremberg Laws, and as a survivor still felt that threat within him, was unable to subscribe to the casual reorganization of history, although he knew that he was striking a now outmoded note. History, "ce mélange indécent de banalité et d'apocalypse,"[11] remained terrible and horrible to him, and he stood firm by his position. The essay in which, under the title "An den Grenzen des Geistes" ("At the Mind's Limits"), Améry describes his life as a slave laborer in Auschwitz-Monowitz affirms the utter helplessness of human beings before the objective lunacy of history: "That is the way it is. One had fallen under its wheel, and doffed one's cap when a murderer came along."[12] In the same passage he writes: "The power structure of the SS state towered up before the prisoner monstrously and insuperably, a reality that could not be escaped and that therefore finally seemed *reasonable*. No matter what his thinking may have been on the outside, in this sense here he became a Hegelian: in the metallic brilliance of its totality the SS state appeared as a state in which the idea was becoming reality."[13] Because of the apostasy thus forced on him, even later Améry no longer trusted his own trade. "The intellectual," he writes, almost with the heretical approach of Thomas Bernhard, "always and everywhere has been totally under the sway of power. He was, and is, accustomed to doubt it intellectually, to subject it to his critical analysis—and yet in the same intellectual process to capitulate to it."[14] Writing, such is the résumé of a terrible apprenticeship, is a dubious business, merely more grist to the mill. And yet, considering the superior force of objectivity, it is even less defensible to refrain from writing than to go on with it, however senseless it may seem.

One of the most impressive aspects of Améry's stance as a writer is that although he knew the real limits of the power to resist as few others did, he maintains the validity of resistance even to the point of absurdity. Resistance without any confidence that it will be effective, resistance *quand même,* out of a principle of solidarity with victims and as a deliberate affront to those who simply let the stream of history sweep them along, is the essence of Améry's philosophy. It is intentionally associated with French existentialism, in no way related to the existentialism propagated as an apologia in postwar German culture, which Améry regarded as opportunistic and contemptible. The existentialist philosophical position adopted by Améry, taking his guidelines from Sartre, makes no concessions to history but exemplifies the necessity of continuing to protest, a dimension so strikingly lacking from German postwar literature. "Where there is a common bond between me and the world, whose unrevoked death sentence I acknowledge as a social reality, it dissolves in polemics. You don't want to listen? Listen anyhow. You don't want to know to where your indifference can again lead you and me at any time? I'll tell you."[15]

The energy behind Améry's polemics derived from implacable resentment. A large number of his essays are concerned with justifying this emotion (commonly regarded as a warped need for revenge) as essential to a truly critical view of the past. Resentment, writes Améry in full awareness of the illogicality of his attempt at definition, "nails every one of us onto the cross of his ruined past. Absurdly, it demands that the irreversible be turned around, that the event be undone."[16] He stands by this absurdity, recognizing its bias and regarding it as evidence that the "moral truth"[17] of the conflict in which he finds himself is to be seen not in any readiness for reconciliation but in the unremitting denunciation of injustice. Nothing is further from Améry's mind than the idea that he could "be compensated for my suffering,"[18] although he allows himself to speculate that the Flemish SS man Wajs who had hit him on the head with a shovel handle understood the moral truth of his misdeeds when he stood before the firing squad. "At that moment he was with *me*—and I was no longer alone with the shovel handle. I would like to believe that at the instant of his execution he wanted exactly as much as I to turn back time, to undo what had been done. When they led him to the place of execution, the antiman had once again become a fellow man."[19] Even with his reservation, expressed in the subjunctive mood—"I would like to believe"—Améry casts doubt on his conjecture, although its plausibility cannot be dismissed entirely. Clearly, when Améry puts his resentment to the test in this example he is concerned not with the SS man's moral "enlightenment," and therefore something like the reintroduction of the *jus talionis,* but, as in every line he wrote, with an attempt to actualize the conflict—which never in the moral sense took place— between the overpowered and those who overpowered them. As Améry pointed out, that actualization could not "consist in a revenge dealt out in proportion to what was suffered."[20] Améry believes as little in the possibility of revenge as in the idea of atonement, which he describes as dubious from the outset: at the most, he considers it of theological significance and therefore irrelevant to him. The issue, then, is not to resolve but to reveal the conflict. The spur of resentment which Améry conveys to us in his polemic demands recognition of the *right* to resentment, entailing no less than a programmatic attempt to sensitize the consciousness of a people "already rehabilitated by time." The "extravagant moral daydream" to which Améry abandons himself in pursuit of such ideas would, he says—if the demand came from the German people themselves—have "tremendous weight, enough so that by this alone it would already be fulfilled. The German revolution would be made good, Hitler disowned."[21]

With such hypotheses about the voluntary reformation of a nation, which he finds at least conceivable, Améry moves out into a region of what, for him, is almost Utopian optimism. He imagines a country where even the victims can live again, and envisages the restitution of the lost homeland that so occupied his mind. The high degree of personal commitment with which he puts his case here can be understood only if we try to assess the specific significance to Améry of his origins in the Austrian provinces. Vorarlberg, where the Mayer family had lived for generations, and the Salzkammergut, where Améry grew up, provided a background to emigration and exile which was qualitatively different in nature from such places as Berlin or Vienna. Our conditioned ignorance of these things still makes it seem somehow improbable that the Nuremberg Laws applied not only to the Jewish communities of major cities, seen to some extent as abstract entities, but to a young Jew from Gmunden whose father had fallen in the First World War as a Tyrolean Imperial Rifleman, a young man who, as Améry admits, had not yet emerged from his own Austrocentric idea of the world and was at best acquainted with mediocre Austrian literature striking a note of local patriotism.[22] The process of degradation initiated by the Nuremberg Laws must have seemed all the worse to Améry because it found him unprepared. He had not grown up feeling that persecution was only temporarily in abeyance, he did not know the deep sense of difference imposed on even the most willingly assimilated Jews by their assimilated environment, a phenomenon noted in so many Jewish autobiographies. He truly thought himself at home. "One warm summer evening," Améry writes of himself in his volume *Örtlichkeiten* ("Localities"), "he is walking through the woods of the Rax region with a friend, looks out over the Semmering mountain range immortalized by Peter Altenberg, sentimentally puts an arm round his companion's shoulders and says: No one will get us away from here."[23] The illusion of security conjured up in these lines later becomes the gauge of his disillusionment. When, at the darkest hour, a Polish Jew asks Améry where he comes from—"V'n wie kimt Ihr?"—he cannot give a proper answer.[24] Vilnius might have made sense, or Amsterdam. But what was the Polish Jew, "for whom wandering and expulsion were just as much family history as for me a permanence of abode that had become meaningless,"[25] to make of a reference to Hohenems or Gmunden? The territory he took most for granted had become a more impossible point of reference than the most outlandish of places. Améry recalls that he had been unable to imagine the idiocy of anti-Semitism, which he had of course encountered in Vienna in the years before his exile, spreading to his own province. As a result the destruction of his home by Fascism, something also lamented by Heinrich Böll and Ingeborg Bachmann, must have had an even more drastic effect on Améry. "Everything that had filled my consciousness—from the history of my country, which was no longer mine, to the landscape images, whose memory I suppressed—had become intolerable to me since that morning of the 12 of March 1938, on which the blood-red cloth with the black spider on a white field had waved even from the windows of out-of-the-way farmsteads. I was a person who could no longer say 'we' and who therefore said 'I' merely out of habit, but not with the feeling of full possession of myself."[26] The destruction of someone's native land is as one with that person's destruction. Separation becomes déchirure [a rending], and there can be no new homeland. "Home is the land of one's childhood and youth. Whoever has lost it remains lost himself, even if he has learned not to stumble about in the foreign country as if he were drunk."[27] The *mal du pays* to which Améry confesses, although he wants no more to do with that particular *pays*—in this connection he quotes a dialect maxim, "In a Wirthaus, aus dem ma aussigschmissn worn is, geht ma nimmer eini" ("When you've been thrown out of an inn you never go back")—is, as Cioran commented, one of the most persistent symptoms of our yearning for security. "Toute nostalgie," he writes, "est un dépassement du présent. Même sous la forme du regret, elle prend un caractère dynamique: on veut forcer le passé, agir rétro-activement, protester contre l'irréversible."[28] To that extent, Améry's homesickness was of course in line with a wish to revise history. When he crossed the border into exile in Belgium, and had to take on himself the Jewish quality of homelessness, of being elsewhere, *être ailleurs,* he did not yet know how hard it would be to endure the tension between his native land as it became ever more foreign and the land of his foreign exile as it became ever more familiar. Seen in this light, Améry's suicide in Salzburg resolved the insoluble conflict between being both at home and in exile, "entre le foyer et le lointain."[29]

For those whose business is language, it is only in language that the unhappiness of exile can be overcome. In his essays on aging, published in 1968, Améry says that "maybe he should have worked with great exertion in the years after 1945 on nothing else but developing his language."[30] But after his liberation from the camps he found himself unable to do even that. "It was a long time," he writes, "before we were able even to learn the ordinary language of freedom. Still today, incidentally, we speak it with discomfort and without real trust in its validity."[31] Améry reflected on the crumbling away and dwindling of his mother tongue,[32] and knew that if he wished to say anything about himself he must begin by reconstructing the medium in which his unspoken thoughts moved. The fact that in this difficult plight he, like Peter Weiss, succeeded in operating with a linguistic precision not easily matched in contemporary literature must have given him a freedom denied to him in other areas. But once he had won back his linguistic competence it alone, in his case, was not enough to banish unhappiness entirely. Language is indeed the means whereby he counters the disturbance to his existential equilibrium, but it too ultimately proves inadequate as a cure for the precarious condition of a man losing faith in the world again daily when, on getting up, he sees his Auschwitz number tattooed on his forearm. "La conscience du malheur est une maladie trop grave pour figurer dans une arithmétique des agonies ou dans les registres de l'Incurable."[33] The words that Améry set down on paper, and which seem to *us* full of the comfort of lucidity, to him merely outlined his own incurable malady and drew a dividing line between "deux mondes incommunicables . . . entre l'homme qui a le sentiment de la mort et celui qui ne l'a point," between one man "qui ne meurt qu'un instant" and another "qui ne cesse de mourir."[34] Seen in this light, the act of writing becomes both liberation and the annulment of *délivrance*, the moment in which a man who has escaped death must recognize that he is no longer alive.

Existence prolonged beyond the experience of death has its affective center in a sense of guilt, the guilt of the survivor, which Niederland describes as the worst psychological burden weighing on those of his patients who had escaped being murdered. It is a particularly macabre irony, as Niederland says, that the survivors and not those who committed Nazi crimes should bear the burden of such guilt. Trapped in a feeling of "being overpowered and reduced," plagued by constant "personal discomfort, states of depression and apathetic withdrawal," these surviving victims carry in them a permanent "deep scar left by the *encounter with death* in its most terrible forms."[35] Towards the end of his essays on aging, Améry remembers how he saw "those like him depart in just about every conceivable way. His comrades (one cannot express it otherwise) had *croaked*, as it turned out exactly, from typhus, dysentery, hunger, from the blows with which they were tortured, even snapping for breath in Zyklon B."[36] Among the irreversible consequences of this kind of horror, past which, as Améry remarks, one had to walk ignoring it, was that the survivor's mind was marked by a "chronologically conditioned engram of death,"[37] and also, somatically, by a long sequence of severe afflictions listed by Niederland in his analyses: psychomotor disturbance, organic brain damage; disorders of the heart, circulation, and digestion; a decrease in general vitality; and premature aging. Apart from Niederland's professional case histories, which show that humiliation of the victim continued even in the compensation proceedings, only Améry's writings give an adequate idea of what it means to have been delivered up to death.

It becomes retrospectively clear that in the linguistic confrontation with his terrible past which filled the last fifteen years of his life Améry, who on various occasions questioned his own courage, was conducting a heroic rearguard action. The insight he acquired from it was "that the discourse of suicide begins where psychology ends,"[38] and relates solely to "pure negation" and "the damnably unimaginable."[39] Améry conceived of this discourse as the last phase of a tedious "bowing down, approaching the earth, a summary of the many humiliations which the suicide's dignity and humanity will not accept."[40] Undoubtedly the author of this essay on suicide would have subscribed to the thesis of Cioran, who thought along similar lines and believed that to continue living was made possible only "par les déficiences de notre imagination et de notre mémoire."[41] It is not surprising that he himself, going back over the past in his sad recall of what had been, reached the point where he felt a wish to bring his life to a (nonviolent) end "with a little pin," as he remarks, quoting Shakespeare.

However, at no time did Améry see his death wish, that quintessence of *acedia cordis,* as a reason for resignation to his fate. Rather, it motivated him to maintain his protest. His essay in the form of a novel, *Lefeu oder der Abbruch* ("Lefeu, or Demolition"), published in 1974, is intractable in tone. At the center of this semi-fictional, semi-autobiographical work is a painter no longer willing or able to adapt, *un raté* who will have no more to do with those around him. This man, called Lefeu, real name Feuermann, had been deported to Germany at the time of the Third Reich as a slave laborer, and there witnessed the way in which human beings fell through the trapdoor opened by Hitler "into the void of their negation."[42] Like Mayer-Améry, Feuermann-Lefeu survives, but that is all. To Lefeu survival means condemnation to an existence like that of the lemures, for in his true form he is still an inhabitant of the city of the dead. Primo Levi, Améry's companion for a time in Auschwitz, gave a very concrete description of that city; the Babylonian conglomeration was called Buna, and besides the German managers and technicians it contained forty thousand workers speaking more than twenty languages and brought in from the surrounding camps. The carbide tower built there by the slaves, emblem of the city, rose in its midst, the top of the tower almost always hidden in mist.[43] And in that city, where as we now know not so much as a pound of synthetic rubber was ever produced, we find ourselves, if the metaphor is permissible, in that infernal region where, as Dante says, the wanderer sees a banner "whirling with aimless speed" and followed, he writes, by the dead, "so many that I wondered / how death could have undone so great a number."[44] Améry's representative Lefeu shares with Dante's wanderer a sense of astonishment at the manifest power of death. Lefeu is an allegorical figure— Feuermann, Feiermann, Feyermann, suggesting ideas of fire and of celebration (*Feier* in German). His experience goes far beyond this life. He is a pyromaniac who sits on the outskirts of the forest and stares down on the city through the night, imagining as he does so an artifact entitled "Paris brûle," the creation of a sea of flames. The idea that emerges here is of finding release by engaging in violence himself, and Améry, inspired by Frantz Fanon, thought of it repeatedly. He wondered how it could be that he, a man of the Resistance whose production and distribution of illegal literature in the cause of agitation nearly cost him his life, "could never quite get over not having fought the oppressor *with weapon in hand*."[45] The renunciation of violence, the impossibility of seeing his way clear to violence in the face of the utmost provocation, is one of the sources of Améry's difficulty; consequently, he identified experimentally with Feuermann, the "fireman" who carries the image of the blazing city in his head. Fire, the perfect medium of the force of divine retribution, is ultimately the true passion of the arsonist, here indulging in a revolutionary fantasy: he, Lefeu, is the fire in his own person, and so devours himself as fire does.

The Remorse of the Heart

On *Memory and Cruelty in
the Work of Peter Weiss*

L'HOMME A DES ENDROITS
DE SON PAUVRE COEUR
QUI N'EXISTENT PAS ENCORE
ET OÙ LA DOULEUR ENTRE
AFIN QU'ILS SOIENT.

Léon Bloy

Peter Weiss's picture *der hausierer* ("the Peddler"), painted in 1940, shows a dark industrial landscape rising in the middle ground. Encamped in front of it is a small circus which lends the whole scene a curiously allegorical tone. To one side of the painting and in the foreground, his back half-turned to the viewer and looking over his shoulder as if in farewell, stands a young man with a kind of peddler's tray and a staff. He may have a long journey behind him, and he is obviously about to go down a steep path towards a tent; its opening is both the lightest and the darkest part of the picture. The white fabric of the tent, illuminated by the setting sun, surrounds the complete darkness of its interior, apparently a black space to which the homeless figure shown here at the beginning of his path through life is irresistibly drawn. This self-portrait expresses the artist's need to enter the dwellings of those who no longer live in the light of day, and shows him intent upon his own end, for even later, with persistence bordering on monomania, Weiss remained faithful to the program it presents. All his work is designed as a visit to the dead: first his own dead, his sister who died so sadly young and who haunted his mind; Uli, the friend of his youth, whose corpse was washed up on the Danish shore in 1940; his parents, to whom he never entirely said good-bye; and then all the other victims of history who are now dust and ashes. In a sustained rhapsodic passage in his 1970 notebook, Weiss writes of the meetings he must have with the dead, and his solidarity with those who already "only too obviously bear [their death] around with them, who are on the way to the ferryboat, to Acheron, who already hear Charon's call and the plashing of his oars."[1] The process of writing which Weiss has recently planned, now that he is about to embark on his literary work *Ästhetik des Widerstands* ("Aesthetic of Resistance"), is the struggle against "the art of forgetting,"[2] a struggle that is as much part of life as melancholy is of death, a struggle consisting in the constant transfer of recollection into written signs. Despite our fits of "absence" and "weakness," writing is an attempt "to preserve our equilibrium among the living with all our dead within us, as we lament the dead and with our own death before our eyes,"[3] in order to set memory to work, since it alone justifies survival in the shadow of a mountain of guilt. More clearly than the oeuvre of any other contemporary author, the writings of Peter Weiss show that abstract memory of the dead is of little avail against the lure of waning memory if it does not also express sympathy—sympathy going beyond mere pity—in the study and reconstruction of an actual time of torment. The artistic self also engages personally in such a reconstruction, pledging itself, as Weiss sees it, to set up a memorial, and the painful nature of that process could be said to ensure the continuance of memory.

Accordingly, there are many depictions of the most cruel procedures even in the pictures created during the first years of Weiss's exile, works that he constructed on the basis of a moral impulse, showing no aesthetic extravagance in any form, and sometimes leading into scenarios depicting the general decline of a civilization brought, in its new barbarism, to conceive of such ideas. *Das grosse Welttheater* ("The Great World Theater") of 1937, which in its pathological chromaticism and the cosmic sweep of its design directly suggests Altdorfer's *Alexanderschlacht* ("Battle of Alexander"), portrays a pandemonium of transgression in front of a background of capsizing ships and lit by the reflection of a conflagration. It is true that the concept of catastrophe developed by Weiss in such panoramas opens up no eschatological perspective; rather, it denotes a now permanent state of destruction. What is seen, here and now, is already an underworld beyond anything natural, a surreal region of industrial complexes and machines, chimneys, silos, viaducts, walls, labyrinths, leafless trees, and cheap fairground attractions, in which the protagonists, scarcely alive anymore, exist as wholly autistic beings without any past history. The figures with lowered eyelids in the *Gartenkonzert* ("Concert in the Garden"), painted in 1938, including the young harpsichordist with his blind gaze, are among the harbingers of a life surviving at best only in the sensation of pain, in unreserved identification with the despised, scorned, crippled, and fading, with those who sit weeping in their places of concealment, who have given up everything and left nothing behind.[4] The incurable melancholy into which the narrator's mother lapses in the third volume of *Die Ästhetik des Widerstands* when, on her wanderings through the eastern provinces of the Reich of the time, she involuntarily surrenders to the fate of those who "robbed of all claims, robbed of all dignity, exist only in a world consisting of loading areas, transport lines, transit points, and reception camps,"[5] a state of utterly silent melancholia in which, as he notes, his mother was irretrievably "removed from everything with which we have surrounded ourselves,"[6] and never uttered so much as a sound of distress, leads her son to wonder as he writes this account whether, having lost her reason in the

Oświęcim region, she "does not know more than we who are still sane,"[7] and whether, as he says in the notebooks, "silence and surrender would not be more honest than the urge to erect our own memorial in our lifetime."[8] The scruples of articulation thus outlined in the face of the most profound destruction were already Weiss's subject in the self-portraits from his sad period of exile. A gouache of 1946 shows a face marked by deep melancholy, while a portrait executed at about the same time in cold shades of blue is striking for its huge sense of concentrated intellectual resilience. Here a scrutinizing eye intent on truth and justice is immediately and steadfastly directed out of the picture and towards what the artist wants it to register. In common to both portraits, however, is the way the painter captures his own physiognomy, with less concern for realistic fidelity of detail than for surface depiction which already shows that touch of monumental heroism characteristic of his late literary works. The transformation of the wounded subject into another, intransigent person constitutes itself as both the will to resist and a process that may be described as the assimilation of the chill of the system which the subject knows threatens him. The fear of being dissected and mutilated is thus transformed into the generative factor in a strategy whereby Weiss himself maintains his intention of dissecting the incarnate authorities of an oppressive reality in order to study them. The subject of anatomy, which interested him in many ways both then and later, is one of the themes illustrating the process of transference involved here, a process which in many ways is very problematical.

One of Peter Weiss's earliest nightmares was the idea of being slaughtered. The two men with knives who, as he writes in *Abschied von den Eltern* ("Farewell to My Parents"), are coming towards him out of a dark gateway—in the background, the pig on which they have just been working lies on a pile of branches—are the envoys of a superior power to which the child already feels he has been delivered up, and whose agents he recognizes in all figures of authority, but more particularly doctors, who obviously have a professional interest in invading his body. At the heart of this entire complex of themes there undoubtedly lies panic terror of an execution that will inflict further destruction, even after death, on the guilty victim's body. It is a central insight in Peter Weiss's work that he diagnoses this process not merely as a legal measure in those societies which make a public festival of capital punishment, an example being the execution of Damien as described by de Sade, but points out that even (and indeed more particularly) "enlightened" civilizations have not abandoned that most drastic form of penalty which consists of cutting up and disemboweling the human body, thus literally making detritus of it. The fact that it is done for some other reason, for instance in the service of medical science, makes little difference to the process itself. In the anatomical picture painted by Weiss in 1946, an apparently headless corpse lies on the dissecting table. The organs removed from it are already resting in various cubic and cylindrical containers, to be taken away for whatever further purpose awaits them. The gravity of the moment can be read in the expressions on the faces of the three male figures who have taken up position, in contemplative attitudes, beside the victim of the procedure that has just been carried out. This is no longer the public spectacle, sanctified by society's legal system, of the destruction of a human body found guilty, while Casanova slips his hand under the skirt of a lady watching the entertainment with him. The ritual performed on the victim in Weiss's picture derives from inspiration of a more recent kind which, in a spirit of the general maintenance of order, aims for the fullest possible identification and labeling of all the separate parts of a corporeality increasingly seen as subversive. However, it is hard to make out exactly what the three strange watchers by the dead body represent. Are they, as we might assume from the composition of the picture, giving prominence to their strikingly clean hands, the dissectors themselves pausing for a rest? Are they, as the classical costumes suggest, priestly augurs or—as at least the Socratic head of one of the three figures may imply—philosophers, taking the body apart out of a love of the truth? At any rate, it is obvious that this dissection, as indicated by the bearing of the three men and the blind indifference of their eyes, which no longer even perceive the dissected body, was performed not in the service of vengeful jurisdiction but of some other idea, some neutral principle of knowledge, and is justified by the purpose or value extrapolated, by a new professional attitude, from the suffering of a created being. A striking feature of another work of art on an anatomical subject, the famous picture painted by Rembrandt van Rijn early in the bourgeois era, is the way in which none of the surgeons present at Dr. Nicolaes Tulp's demonstration is looking at the body of the poor thief Aris Kindt of Leyden, here shown under the knife; instead, all eyes are bent on the open textbook of anatomy, lest they be overwhelmed by the fascination of the business. Rembrandt's picture of the dissection of a hanged body in the interests of higher ideals is an unsettling comment on the particular kind of knowledge to which we owe progress. In Peter Weiss's much more primitive anatomical picture one cannot be certain whether the painter imagined himself subjected to the procedure he shows, or whether, like Descartes (known to have been an enthusiastic amateur surgeon who in all historical probability attended several of Dr. Tulp's anatomy lessons), he thought that he could discover the secret of the human machine in the dissection of bodies, a subject to which he returns again and again. A picture of a dissection done two years earlier, showing an anatomist who appears both far more humane and far more cruel, with a knife in his right hand, an organ he has removed in his left, and bending over the human body he has opened up with an expression of utter desolation, does not entirely rule out the possibility that Peter Weiss felt a certain morbid interest in the process and identified with the anatomist. Noteworthy in this connection are those passages of the *Ästhetik des Widerstands* in which Weiss, with much stronger commitment than in the political sections of his work, describes the history of the painter Théodore Géricault who, as the author interprets it, immersed himself "in the study of dead skin . . . in the morgue,"[9] because "he wanted to intervene in the system of suppression and destruction."[10] The political theme that Weiss brings to the fore here, as he does throughout the *Ästhetik des Widerstands,* is admittedly contradicted by the motivation which ultimately determines the effect made by a work of art: the fact that physicality is most strongly sculpted and its "nature" most perceptible on the indistinct borderline with transcendency.[11] Such an affinity with the dead, impelled by a desire for knowledge but also implying a libidinous occupation of the dissected body, makes one suspect that the handling of paint in a case like Géricault's, an example of the extremist practice of art to which Weiss too subscribes, is ultimately equivalent to an attempt by the subject, horrified as he is by human life, to do away with himself through successive acts of destruction. Seen from this viewpoint, the darkly massive work of Théodore Géricault, into which the first-person narrator of the *Ästhetik des Widerstands* transfers himself because it seems to him to represent every level on which "the unendurability of life has its roots,"[12] would correspond to the text of the *Ästhetik* itself, that genuinely catastrophic novel in which, with a shattering sense of system, Peter Weiss wrecked what he knew was the little life remaining to him.

In 1963 Weiss noted that he could say many of his works dated from his childhood,[13] a remark that certainly applies to his subsequent writings and suggests the etiology of the compulsion under which he wrote. In *Abschied von den Eltern* he produced, relatively early in his oeuvre, an exemplary study of the forgotten or repressed sorrows and passions of his childhood. Psychoanalysis had helped him to uncover them. The curious collage accompanying the text provides an iconographic parallel: it shows a portrait of a thoughtful boy in a sailor suit digging with a little spade on a patch of wasteland, in front of an architectural background of factories and ecclesiastical buildings. His archaeological excavation of childhood begins, typically, with his memory of his father's death. Weiss describes seeing his father lying in his coffin, in a black suit now much too large for him. He notices in the dead man "something proud and bold that I had never before perceived,"[14] and strokes "the cold, sallow, taut skin of the hand"[15]—a symbolic gesture whereby he not only assures himself that his father is really dead but also undertakes to continue, in his own future, with the "constant efforts"[16] his parent had made while he was alive, as if that task were incumbent on him. In some societies, we are told, when a father dies the son takes an imprint of his hand and thus, in a final act of internalization, authority passes entirely into the bereaved son. Years later, in a note which cannot be explained by any other context, Weiss once again recalls "my father's great exertions," as if not to forget them. "First emigrated after the First World War, from Vienna to Germany. In 1934 went from Germany to England. In 1936 to the Czech Socialist Republic. In 1938 emigrated again, to Sweden, beginning a new life at the age of 53. . . . And he had already been so ill in England."[17] The son, who began too late on *his* work and feels that he has always "wasted" time, cannot lag behind. His father's great exertions are the example he must now follow. The figure of his father as the supreme moral authority lives on in the passing of judgment. The force motivating the equally great exertions made by Weiss himself in the work of his last decades thus, in spite of the insights revealed to him by psychoanalysis, remains the ever-present fear of punishment to which he was exposed as a child. The illustrations to the Grimms' fairytales and in particular the naïve, brightly colored pictures of *Struwwelpeter,* which seem to him like scenes from his own dreams—and not just because his name enables him to identify with the title figure—assume a central position in this excavation of what, as Weiss often stressed later, was a terrible childhood. Harriet, who goes up in flames because she cannot keep her hands off the matchbox; the punishment of Frederick, who torments animals and has to go to bed when a dog bites his leg and makes it bleed (the doctor, who has a big stick, gives him bitter medicine while the dog eats his sausage); the sexually indeterminate, anorexic Augustus, whose death wish makes him refuse his soup; the tailor's huge scissors and Conrad's amputated thumbs—all these are archetypes in which the child, and later the apparently sophisticated adult, perceives the horror of execution. It is in the nature of the judicial code of this picture-book world of cautionary tales for naughty children that the reader for whom they are intended cannot take his eyes off them. They are truly unforgettable, and their power and effect are only reinforced when the child goes on to read other tales of torture, robbery, arson, and murder. From one particularly gruesome story, in which soldiers bind their Indian prisoners to the mouths of cannon, he even learns that some kinds of death penalty destroy the soul as well as the body. The child is on familiar terms with the curious moral knowledge thus acquired, even in its most sinister aspect: he takes a perverse pleasure in its specifically German form of didactic cruelty.

Peter Weiss the rigorous moralist had his early schooling in the fantastic depiction of all imaginable punishments. These acts of mutilation and amputation can be interpreted as pendants to the categorical imperative of memory. Their constant presence ensures the suspension of that active forgetting which Nietzsche, in the *Genealogie der Moral* ("Genealogy of Morality"), called the doorkeeper of mental peace and order.[18] Because there is something to be remembered, Weiss embarks on his literary work and enters purgatory. On the threshold stands that angel who also incises the letter "P," for *peccatum,* on Dante's brow with the point of his sword, in token of the consciousness of sin. The task here imposed on the person who is to be disciplined, as the way to an understanding of his true condition, is to elicit the significance of the letter carved in the skin by patient endurance of the pain—an archaic ordeal on the same principles as those behind the construction of that notorious instrument of torture discovered by the visitor to a penal colony to have been devised by a former and now discredited governor. "Perhaps," writes Nietzsche in the *Genealogie der Moral,* "there is nothing more terrible and mysterious in the whole prehistory of mankind than our mnemonic technique. We burn something into the mind so that it will remain in the memory; only what still hurts will be retained."[19] To Weiss who, like all moralists, embodies the neurasthenic type apostrophized in Nietzsche's study, memory logically consists almost inevitably in the recall of past torments. In the process, however, he discovers not only the *partie honteuse* (shameful part) of his own inner life, made up of many diverse and monstrous fantasies—Weiss is the great pornographer *manqué* of modern German literature—but also the objective nature of a society where what really happened far surpassed the most outrageous dreams of annihilation. In his progress as a dramatist, from grisly street ballads to his play on the lurid atrocities of the French Revolution, Peter Weiss surveys an area in which the horror figures of childhood and the leading figures of revolutionary government are all preparing a great bloodbath together. But in the course of this development, even private suffering increasingly merges with a realization that the grotesque deformities of our inner lives have their background and origin in collective social history. It was therefore his early history as a German and a Jew, which he does not explore fully even in his autobiography, that was the deciding factor in causing Weiss to attend the Auschwitz trial in Frankfurt. He may also have been motivated before the event by the hope, never quite extinguished, "that every injury has its *equivalent* somewhere and can be truly compensated for, even if it be through the pain of whoever inflicted the injury." This idea, which Nietzsche thought was the basis of our sense of justice and which, he said, "rests on a contractual relationship between creditor and debtor as old as the concept of law itself,"[20] can of course, in accordance with its own spirit, be put into practice only in an archaic society. In the Frankfurt trial, however, the self-imposed restraint of the civil legal system meant that any real compensation for the victims, in the shape of a kind of "entitlement to cruelty," was out of the question.[21] Instead, the witnesses were subjected yet again to the lengthy torments of remembering, as they were required to do, what they had once endured, while the defendants came off scot-free. Yet it may not have been only this drawback, inherent in the fact that no meaningful or satisfactory legal redress was or could be made at the trial, that induced Weiss to resume the investigation on a literary level after it was over; the task was unavoidable because he realized that the legal process alone could not answer the question, so vital to him, of whether he himself was on the side of the creditors or the debtors. He finds the answer to the question in the course of his own study, as it becomes increasingly clear to him that rulers and ruled, exploiters and exploited are in fact the same species, so that he, the potential victim, must also range himself with the perpetrators of the crime or at least their accomplices, and not just in a purely theoretical sense either. Weiss's willingness to take this heaviest of all moral obligations on himself raises his work far beyond all other literary attempts to "come to terms with the past," as the usual phrase runs. Nowhere, perhaps, is the symbiotic interweaving of this author's personal life with that of Jews *and* Germans so strikingly clear as in the names he gives to some of the agents of cruelty whom he presents on stage. Kaspar Rosenrot in *Nacht mit Gästen* ("Night with Guests") is a mixture of German and Jew, and the names of the Nazi criminals—whether real or invented—Tausendschön, Liebseel, and Gotthilf[*]—which Weiss entered in his notebook in various different versions while he was working on *Die Ermittlung* ("The Investigation")[22] also derive from a history of assimilation which produced the unhappiest of hybrids. The paradigmatic figure here is the deformed Rumpelstiltskin who cannot succeed in tearing himself in half, as Weiss confirms with the deepest self-irony when he writes in his 1964 notebook, "How glad I am that I am not a German."[23] This facile exoneration does not fail to make its point; on the contrary, it shows his awareness that he, once described angrily by his Jewish father as a young rascal of a Jew, is also a German, at least insofar as German ideas of morality prevailed in

---

[*]These names suggest flowers ("Rosenrot" = rose-red), beauty, a loving soul, and divine aid.

his parental home. That relationship dictated his attempt to identify with both the murder victims and the murderers, a delicate undertaking which is given almost paranoid emphasis in the scene in *Die Ermittlung* recapitulating the incident when Klehr, the medical orderly accused in the trial, injects phenol into the heart of a patient condemned to medical execution while two other prisoners assist him by holding the man down. The names of the two ordered to perform this service were, as Witness 6 remembers, Schwarz and Weiss.* In view of such an almost symbolic coincidence, which was certainly incorporated into the text deliberately, any kind of moralizing simplification must be out of the question. Compensation for the subjective sense of personal involvement in genocide, in which the writer's guilt neurosis assumes almost unmanageable proportions, could be made only if he placed the objective social conditions and preconditions of the tragedy at the center of his discourse. And not the least merit of Peter Weiss's *Die Ermittlung,* particularly by comparison with anything else written on the subject by the mid-1960s, lies here, in indicating that even now the economic conditions, considerations, and forms of organization making genocide possible continued to operate. Like Witness 3, he reminds us and himself that we all knew the society giving rise to the regime which could create

*Black and White.

camps where, as he continues, the exploiters were able to develop their dominance to a hitherto unprecedented degree.[24] Mass murder, after all, was no more than an extreme variation on the elimination of human beings by working them to death, as practiced in Germany in the war years on a far greater scale than ever before in history. Alexander Kluge was later to study its specific logic, which was entirely consistent with the system, in his *Neue Geschichten* ("New Stories"). From the viewpoint of the national economy, which even today rules almost everything, the perversion of the Fascist concentration camps consisted not so much in the nature and extent of the crimes committed there as in the fact that the system's economic exploitation of human detritus—Weiss notes the relevant statistics and speaks of the "exploitation even of blood, bones and ashes"[25]—came nowhere even approximately close to justifying the expenditure involved. And there is an almost metaphysical dimension to this negative balance sheet, an apparently entirely aimless evil, which made Weiss try to incorporate its historical experience, with all the authentic details, into the salvation story as exemplified by the tectonic structure of the *Divina Commedia*. Although Weiss could no longer reconstruct Dante's model as a whole in all its significant unity, the transfer of the horrors attendant upon genocide into an aesthetic pattern helps the author to free himself of torment even more than does the rational explanation of its social basis. The mere fact that, in the thirty-three cantos of *Die Ermittlung,* he could describe only the circles of the Inferno is the verdict on a period that has left any hope of salvation far behind.

However, the structure of Dante's world, in which only the northern hemisphere is populated, while the miracles of nature and achievements of civilization cover the misery lying directly beneath that fragile layer, does seem significant insofar as it expresses the intimate relationship between the *historia calamitatum* of mankind and what we derive, in cultural terms, from collective misfortune. The question forcing itself on the reader of the *Commedia*—did not the poet who composed those 14,233 lines of verse keep drawing new inspiration from the idea of the penalties with which he himself was threatened?—also occurs to a reader of the work of Peter Weiss. Dante, banished from his native city on pain of death by fire, was probably in Paris in 1310 when fifty-nine Templars were burned alive on a single day, and, like Dante, Weiss learned in exile to understand the fate he had escaped. This is the justification for the sadomasochistic preoccupation, the repeated and virtuoso representation of suffering, manifest in the literary work of two poets more than half a millennium apart in time, yet very much alike in spirit. In addition, the endemic perversion of cruelty inherent in the history of mankind is always described in the hope that the last chapter in that horror story will be written, and in a better time posterity will be able to look back like the blessed souls in heaven, the *beati in regno coelesti,* of whom Aquinas said that they would be able to watch the spectacle of the torments of the damned *ut beatitudo illis magis complaceat*—so that they might be all the more aware of their own happy condition. The purpose of representing cruelty thus outlined, as we now know, has never been fulfilled and probably never can be, since our species is unable to learn from its mistakes. Consequently such arduous cultural efforts can no more come to a conclusion than the pain and torment they seek to remedy. The torture of those never-ending efforts is the true wheel of Ixion on which the creative imagination is always binding itself again, so that it can at least be absolved in doing penance. The case of Peter Weiss demonstrates, with particular cogency, the attempt to attain absolution in heroic, self-destroying work. His *Ästhetik des Widerstands,* that thousand-page work of fiction which he began when he was well over fifty, making a pilgrimage over the arid slopes of our cultural and contemporary history in the company of *pavor nocturnus,* the terror of the night, and laden with a monstrous weight of ideological ballast, is a magnum opus which sees itself, almost programmatically, not only as the expression of an ephemeral wish for redemption, but as an expression of the *will* to be on the side of the victims at the end of time. As far as I know there is nothing else in literature like the ten-page passage towards the end of the novel describing the murder of the Resistance fighters at Plötzensee by the executioners Röttger and Rosenlieb. It records an accumulated sense of the fear and pain of death, and must almost have exhausted its author; that account is the place from which Weiss, as a writer, does not return. The rest of the text is only a postlude, the coda to a martyrs' chronicle. In the same way as Géricault completed a self-destructive work in his studio in the rue des Martyrs, as a warning to what he saw as a society working destructively on principle, Peter Weiss gained a place in the company of the martyrs of the Resistance in the long paroxysm of his memory. One of the Resistance fighters concludes a farewell letter to his parents—and here again we hear the voice of Peter Weiss—with the words "O Herakles. The light is dim, my pencil blunt. I would have wished to write it all differently. But the time is too short. And I have run out of paper."[26]

Notes

Air War and Literature: Zurich Lectures

1. See H. Glaser, *1945—Ein Lesebuch* (Frankfurt am Main, 1995), pp. 18ff., also Sir Charles Webster and Noble Frankland, *The Strategic Air Offensive Against Germany* (Her Majesty's Stationery Office, 1954–1956), especially vol. IV, containing appendices, statistics, and documents.
2. See Alexander Kluge, *Geschichte und Eigensinn* (Frankfurt am Main, 1981), p. 97.
3. Janet Flanner, in Hans Magnus Enzensberger, *Europa in Trümmern* (Frankfurt am Main, 1990), p. 240.
4. Alfred Döblin, in Enzensberger, op. cit., p. 188.
5. Willi Ruppert, ". . . und Worms lebt dennoch" (Wormser Verlagsdruckerei, n.d.).
6. Robert Thomas Pell, in Enzensberger, op. cit., p. 110.
7. Enzensberger, op. cit., p. 11.
8. Heinrich Böll, *Hierzulande* (Munich, 1963), p. 128.

9. Heinrich Böll, *Der Engel schwieg* (Cologne, 1992).

10. Enzensberger, op. cit., p. 20f.

11. Hans Erich Nossack, "Der Untergang," in *Interview mit dem Tode* (Frankfurt am Main, 1972), p. 209.

12. Max Hastings, *Bomber Command* (London, 1979), p. 346.

13. Quoted in Charles Messenger, *"Bomber" Harris and the Strategic Bombing Offensive 1939–1945* (London, 1984), p. 39.

14. Webster and Frankland, op. cit., vol. IV, p. 144.

15. Albert Speer, *Erinnerungen* (Berlin, 1969), pp. 359ff.

16. Taylor is quoted in Hastings, op. cit., p. 349.

17. See Gerard J. De Groot, "Why Did They Do It?" *The Times Higher Educational Supplement,* October 16, 1992, p. 18.

18. Quoted in ibid.

19. Solly Zuckerman, *From Apes to Warlords* (London, 1978), p. 352.

20. Elaine Scarry, *The Body in Pain* (Oxford, 1985), p. 74.

21. "Raid on Berlin" (September 4, 1943), audiocassette, Imperial War Museum, London.

22. Klaus Schmidt, *Die Brandnacht* (Darmstadt, 1964), p. 61.

23. See Nikolaus Martin, *Prager Winter* (Munich, 1991), p. 234.

24. Friedrich Reck, *Tagebuch eines Verzweifelten* (Frankfurt am Main, 1994), p. 220.

25. Ibid., p. 216.

26. Nossack, op. cit., p. 213.

27. Alexander Kluge, in *Neue Geschichten. Hefte 1–18 "Unheimlichkeit der Zeit"* (Frankfurt am Main, 1977), p. 106.

28. Ibid., p. 104.

29. Victor Klemperer, *Ich will Zeugnis ablegen bis zum letzten— Tagebücher 1942–1945* (Berlin, 1995), pp. 661ff. (English version *To the Bitter End,* tr. Martin Chalmers [London, 1999], pp. 389ff.)

30. Nossack, op. cit., p. 211.

31. Reck, op. cit., p. 216.

32. Ibid., p. 221.

33. Quoted from Enzensberger, op. cit., p. 203f.

34. Ibid., p. 79.

35. Zuckerman, op. cit., p. 322.

36. Nossack, op. cit., pp. 211f. and 226f.

37. Heinrich Böll, *Frankfurter Vorlesungen* (Munich, 1968), p. 82f.

38. Nossack, op. cit., p. 238.

39. Ibid.

40. Böll, *Der Engel schwieg*, p. 138.

41. Quoted in Zuckerman, op. cit., p. 327.

42. Böll, *Der Engel schwieg*, p. 70.

43. Nossack, op. cit., p. 238f.

44. Böll, *Der Engel schwieg*, p. 57.

45. Nossack, op. cit., p. 243.

46. Böll, *Der Engel schwieg*, p. 45f.

47. Stig Dagerman, *German Autumn* (London, 1988), pp. 7ff.

48. Victor Gollancz, *In Darkest Germany* (London, 1947), p. 30.

49. This and the preceding quotation are from Böll, *Der Engel schwieg*, p. 92.

50. See Martin Middlebrook, *The Battle of Hamburg* (London, 1988), p. 359.

51. Kluge, *"Unheimlichkeit der Zeit,"* p. 35.

52. Nossack, op. cit., p. 220.

53. Alexander Kluge, *Theodor Fontane, Heinrich von Kleist, Anna Wilde—Zur Grammatik der Zeit* (Berlin, 1987), p. 23.

54. Schmidt, op. cit., p. 17.

55. Nossack, op. cit., p. 245.

56. Max Frisch, *Tagebücher,* quoted in Enzensberger, op. cit., p. 261.

57. Quoted in Zuckerman, op. cit., p. 192f.

58. Thomas Mann, *Doktor Faustus* (Frankfurt am Main, 1971), p. 433; English version, tr. H. T. Lowe-Porter (London, 1949), p. 434.

59. Hans Erich Nossack, *Pseudoautobiographische Glossen* (Frankfurt am Main, 1971), p. 51.

60. Hermann Kasack, *Die Stadt hinter dem Strom* (Frankfurt am Main, 1978), p. 18.

61. Ibid., p. 10.

62. Nossack, *Pseudoautobiographische Glossen,* p. 62.

63. Kasack, op. cit., p. 152.

64. Ibid., p. 154.

65. Ibid., p. 142.

66. Ibid., p. 315.

67. Cf. Nossack, *Pseudoautobiographische Glossen,* p. 47: "Real literature was a secret language at the time."

68. Nossack, *Untergang,* p. 225.

69. Ibid., p. 217.

70. Ibid., p. 245.

71. Elias Canetti, *Die gespaltene Zukunft* (Munich, 1972), p. 58.

72. Peter de Mendelssohn, *Die Kathedrale* (Hamburg, 1983), p. 10.

73. Ibid., p. 29.

74. Ibid., p. 98.

75. Ibid., p. 234.

76. The quotations in the preceding lines are from ibid., p. 46.

77. Arno Schmidt, *Aus dem Leben eines Fauns* (Frankfurt am Main, 1973), p. 152; English version, *Scenes from the Life of a Faun,* tr. John E. Woods (London and New York, 1983), p. 145.

78. Hubert Fichte, *Detlevs Imitationen "Grünspan"* (Frankfurt am Main, 1982), p. 35; English version, *Detlev's Imitations,* tr. Martin Chalmers (London and New York, 1991).

79. Kluge, *"Unheimlichkeit der Zeit,"* p. 35.

80. Ibid., p. 37.

81. Ibid., p. 39.

82. Ibid., p. 53.

83. Ibid., p. 59.

84. Ibid., p. 63.

85. Ibid., p. 69.

86. Ibid., p. 79.

87. Ibid., p. 102f.

88. Ibid.

89. Walter Benjamin, *Illuminationen* (Frankfurt am Main, 1961), p. 273; English version, *Illuminations,* tr. Harry Zorn (London, 1970).

90. Jörg Friedrich, *Des Gesetz des Krieges* (Munich, 1995).

91. Ed. G. Wolfrum and L. Bröll (Sonthofen, 1963).

92. Günter Jäckel, "Der 13. Februar 1945—Erfahrungen und Reflexionen," *Dresdner Hefte,* no. 41 (1995), p. 3.

93. See Kenzaburo Oe, *Hiroshima Notes* (New York and London, 1997), p. 20.

94. Hans Dieter Schäfer, *Mein Roman über Berlin* (Passau, 1990), p. 27.

95. Ibid., p. 29.

96. Ibid.

97. Hans Dieter Schäfer, *Berlin im zweiten Weltkrieg* (Munich, 1991).

98. Ibid., p. 161.

99. Ibid., p. 164.

100. Franz Lennartz, *Deutsche Schriftsteller des 20. Jahrhundert im Spiegel der Kritik,* vol. 2 (Stuttgart, 1984), p. 1164.

101. See Karl Heinz Janssen, "Der grosse Plan," ZEIT-Dossier, March 7, 1997.

102. See Jäckel, op. cit., p. 6.

103. Quoted in Elias Canetti, op. cit., p. 31f.

104. See Antony Beevor, *Stalingrad* (London, 1998), p. 102ff.

Between the Devil and the Deep Blue Sea:
On Alfred Andersch

1. See ". . . *einmal wirklich leben*"—*Ein Tagebuch in Briefen an Hedwig Andersch 1943–1979,* ed. W. Stephan (Zürich, 1986), p. 70f. In later letters Andersch likes to address his "dear Mama" as "Dear Mom" or "Ma chère maman." What the rather unassuming Frau Andersch made of this we do not know.

2. Ibid., pp. 50, 57, 59, 111, 116, 126, 144.

3. Ibid., p. 123.

4. Hans Werner Richter, *Im Etablissement der Schmetterlinge—Einundzwanzig Portraits aus der Gruppe 47* (Munich, 1988), p. 24.

5. Stephan Reinhardt, *Alfred Andersch, Eine Biographie* (Zürich, 1990), p. 208.

6. Ibid.

7. See E. Schütz, *Alfred Andersch* (Munich, 1980), p. 44f., where the most important reviews are quoted.

8. Koeppel, *Börsenblatt des deutschen Buchhandels,* no. 14 (1966).

9. Marcel Reich-Ranicki, *Sonntagsblatt,* no. 12 (1961).

10. H. Salzinger, *Stuttgarter Zeitung,* October 11, 1967; J. Günther, *Neue Deutsche Hefte,* vol. 14, no. 3 (1967), p. 133f.

11. Reinhardt, op. cit., p. 438.

12. Ibid.

13. Ibid., p. 534.

14. Alfred Andersch, *Die Kirschen der Freiheit,* p. 46.

15. Ibid., p. 43.

16. Ibid., p. 39.

17. Quoted in Reinhardt, op. cit., p. 580.

18. Andersch, *Kirschen der Freiheit,* p. 46.

19. Ibid., p. 45.

20. Reinhardt, op. cit., p. 58.

21. Ibid.

22. Ibid., pp. 55ff.

23. Ibid., p. 84.

24. Ibid., p. 82.

25. See Alfred Andersch, "Der Techniker," in *Erinnerte Gestalten* (Zürich, 1986), pp. 99, 157, 160.

26. Reinhardt, op. cit., p. 647.

27. POW file (October 8, 1944), Archiv der Deutschen Dienststelle, Berlin.

28. Andersch, *Kirschen der Freiheit,* p. 90. And who—so the passage quoted here implies—would want to desert to the losing side?

29. Reinhardt, op. cit., p. 647.

30. See, on this episode Reinhardt, op. cit., p. 73. Andersch referred his company commander to a decree of Hitler's, printed in the information leaflets circulated to the Wehrmacht, providing for the demobilization of former concentration camp inmates.

31. See Andersch, ". . . *einmal wirklich leben,*" p. 20.

32. Ibid.

33. Ibid., p. 47.

34. Ibid.

35. Urs Widmer, *1945 oder die "neue Sprache"* (Pädagogischer Verlag Schwann, Düsseldorf, 1966).

36. *Der Ruf,* ed. H. A. Neunzig (Munich, 1971), p. 21.

37. See M. Overesch, *Chronik deutscher Zeitgeschichte,* vol. 2/III (Düsseldorf, 1983), p. 439f.

38. See *Der Ruf,* p. 26.

39. Alfred Andersch, *Sansibar oder der letzte Grund* (Zürich, 1970), p. 101.

40. Ibid., p. 55.

41. Ibid., p. 59.

42. Ibid., p. 106.

43. Ibid.

44. Ibid., p. 22.

45. Andersch, ". . . *einmal wirklich leben,*" p. 13.

46. Andersch, *Kirschen der Freiheit,* p. 86.

47. Ibid., p. 87.

48. *Die Rote* (Zürich, 1972), p. 152f.

49. Ibid., p. 68.

50. See, for instance, T. Koebner, *Lexikon der deutschsprachigen Gegenwartsliteratur,* ed. H. Kunisch and H. Wiesner (Munich, 1981), p. 26; V. Wehdeking, *Alfred Andersch* (Stuttgart, 1983), p. 91.

51. Alfred Andersch, *Efraim* (Zürich, n.d.), pp. 61, 204, 70, 64, 134.

52. Ibid.

53. Ibid., p. 56.

54. Ibid., p. 152f.

55. Reinhardt, op. cit., p. 423.

56. Alfred Andersch, *Winterspelt* (Zürich, n.d.), p. 39.

57. Ibid., p. 41.

58. Ibid., p. 443.

59. Quoted in Reinhardt, op. cit., p. 327.

60. See ibid., pp. 500, 508.

Against the Irreversible: On Jean Améry

1. Jean Améry, *Jenseits von Schuld und Sühne* (Stuttgart, 1977), p. 68; English translation: *At the Mind's Limits,* trans. Sidney Rosenfeld and Stella D. Rosenfeld (Bloomington, Ind., 1980), p. 36.

2. Ibid., p. 9.

3. W. G. Niederland, *Folgen der Verfolgung—Das Überlebenden-Syndrom* (Frankfurt, 1980), p. 12.

4. Améry, *Jenseits,* p. 15; Eng. p. xiii.

5. Ibid., p. 62f.; Eng. p. 32f.

6. Ibid., p. 63; Eng. p. 33.

7. Ibid., p. 64; Eng. p. 33.

8. This and the preceding quotation: ibid., p. 64; Eng. p. 33f.

9. Ibid., p. 67; Eng. p. 35f.

10. Ibid., p. 66; Eng. p. 35.

11. E. M. Cioran, *Précis de Décomposition* (Paris, 1949), p. 11.

12. Améry, *Jenseits,* p. 33; Eng. p. 11f.

13. Ibid., p. 33; Eng. p. 12.

14. Ibid.

15. Ibid., p. 149; Eng. p. 96.

16. Ibid., p. 149; Eng. p. 68.

17. Ibid., p. 113; Eng. p. 70.

18. Ibid., p. 112; Eng. p. 69.

19. Ibid., p. 114; Eng. p. 70.

20. Ibid., p. 123; Eng. p. 77.

21. This and the two preceding passages are quoted from *Jean Améry, Örtlichkeiten* (Stuttgart, 1980), p. 25.

22. See Améry, *Jenseits,* p. 78; Eng. p. 46.

23. Améry, *Örtlichkeiten.*

24. Ibid., p. 77f.; Eng. p. 44.

25. Ibid.

26. Ibid., p. 75; Eng. p. 43f.

27. Ibid., p. 84; Eng. p. 48.

28. Cioran, op. cit., 49.

29. Ibid., p. 50.

30. Jean Améry, *Über das Altern* (Stuttgart, 1968), p. 30; *On Aging,* trans. John D. Barlow (Bloomington, Ind., 1994), p. 30.

31. Améry, *Jenseits,* p. 44; Eng. p. 20.

32. See ibid., p. 89; Eng. p. 52.

33. Cioran, op. cit., p. 46.

34. Ibid., p. 21.

35. Niederland, op. cit., p. 232.

36. Améry, *Über das Altern,* p. 123; Eng. p. 123.

37. Ibid.

38. Jean Améry, *Hand an sich legen* (Stuttgart, 1976), p. 27.

39. Ibid., p. 30.

40. Ibid., p. 83.

41. Cioran, op. cit., p. 43.

42. Jean Améry, *Lefeu oder der Abbruch* (Stuttgart, 1976), p. 186.

43. Primo Levi, *Si questo è un uomo* (Milan, 1958); English translation: *Survival in Auschwitz* [and *The Reawakening*], transl. Stuart Woolf (New York, 1986).

44. *Divina Commedia,* Inferno, Canto III.

45. Jean Améry, *Widersprüche* (Stuttgart, 1971), p. 157.

The Remorse of the Heart:
On Memory and Cruelty in the Work of Peter Weiss

1. Peter Weiss, *Notizbücher 1960–1971* (Frankfurt, 1982), vol. II, p. 812.
2. Ibid., p. 813.
3. Ibid.
4. Paraphrase of a passage on p. 810 of the *Notizbücher 1960–1971*.
5. Peter Weiss, *Die Ästhetik des Widerstands* (Frankfurt, 1983), vol. III, p. 14.
6. Ibid., p. 16.
7. Ibid.
8. Weiss, *Notizbücher 1960–1971*, vol. II, p. 812.
9. Weiss, *Die Ästhetik des Widerstands*, vol. II, p. 31.
10. Ibid., p. 33.
11. See ibid., p. 31.
12. Ibid.
13. Weiss, *Notizbücher 1960–1971*, vol. I, p. 191.
14. Peter Weiss, *Abschied von den Eltern* (Frankfurt, 1964), p. 8.
15. Ibid.
16. Ibid., p. 9.
17. Weiss, *Notizbücher 1960–1971*, vol. I, p. 58.
18. Friedrich Nietzsche, *Werke*, vol. VI, part 2 (Berlin, 1968), p. 307f.
19. Ibid., p. 311.
20. Ibid., p. 314.
21. Ibid., p. 316.
22. See Weiss, *Notizbücher 1960–1971*, vol. I, pp. 220, 230.
23. Ibid., p. 351.
24. Peter Weiss, *Die Ermittlung* (Frankfurt, 1965), p. 89.
25. Weiss, *Notizbücher 1960–1971*, vol. I, p. 316.
26. Weiss, *Die Ästhetik des Widerstands*, vol. III, p. 210.

About the Author

W. G. SEBALD was born in Wertach im Allgäu, Germany, in 1944. He studied German language and literature in Freiburg, Switzerland, and in Manchester. He taught at the University of East Anglia in Norwich, England, for thirty years, becoming professor of European literature in 1987, and from 1989 to 1994 was the first director of the British Centre for Literary Translation. His previous books—*After Nature, The Rings of Saturn, The Emigrants, Vertigo,* and *Austerlitz*—have won a number of international awards, including the National Book Critics Circle Award, the *L.A. Times* Book Award, the Berlin Literature Prize, and the Literatur Nord Prize. He died in December 2001.

About the Translator

ANTHEA BELL was born in Suffolk and educated at Somerville College, Oxford. She has worked as a translator for many years, primarily from German and French, and her translations include works of nonfiction (biography, politics, social history, musicology, and art history), literary and popular fiction, and classic German works for young people. Anthea Bell has also served on the committee of the Translators Association and the jury panel of the Schlegel-Tieck German translation prize in the U.K., and has received a number of translation prizes and awards, including, in 2002, the Independent Foreign Fiction Prize (U.K.) and the Helen and Kurt Wolff Prize (U.S.) for W. G. Sebald's *Austerlitz*. She lives in Cambridge, England.

About the Type

This book was set in Perpetua, a typeface designed by the English artist Eric Gill, and cut by the Monotype Corporation between 1928 and 1930. Perpetua is a contemporary face of original design, without any direct historical antecedents. The shapes of the roman letters are derived from the techniques of stonecutting. The larger display sizes are extremely elegant and form a most distinguished series of inscriptional letters.